SEND HER QUICKLY TO HER FATE

1. INTRODUCTION

Regardless of an individuals opinion on the rights and wrongs of Capital Punishment, most would agree that the subject is usually considered entirely in a male context and that the very idea of executing a woman is perhaps unthinkable, possibly abhorrent to our modern sensitivities. Yet between 1900 and 1955, Britain is known to have executed 27 women at home and abroad, with perhaps many hundreds more suffering a similar fate in previous centuries.

The most common method of Capital Punishment employed by the British courts during our country's long history has been the public or private hanging of convicted people, although prior to 1874, it would have been more accurately described as "judicial strangling". Public executioners such as William Calcraft who operated between 1829 and 1874 would have typically employed a "short drop" to suspend people by the neck, a method which resulted in most prisoners being slowly asphyxiated to death while they were still temporarily conscious. One male prisoner, who was revived after suffering one of these judicial hangings in Britain, described the extremely painful nature of this particular method of execution, relating how his "spirits" departed his body and the excruciating pain finally passing away as he lapsed into unconsciousness, only to return as he was later revived.

There is also some evidence from modern day executions, in countries that still employ this "short drop" method of judicial hanging that women prisoners who are subjected to this form of punishment, typically survive and struggle longer on the rope, than do their male counterparts. Whether or not this is simply accounted for by a weight differential between the genders is unclear, but generally most prisoners executed in this fashion take around 15 minutes to die, during which time the condemned person is seen to desperately struggle for the life giving breath which is being denied them.

It was another British executioner, William Marwood, operating between 1874 and 1883 that has largely been credited with introducing the much more effective and humane "long drop" which became the common method of execution in Britain. Thought to have first been devised by Irish doctors, this method rendered the condemned prisoner unconscious and at the same time immobilised them by breaking their neck and severing the spinal chord. Although the prisoner was still asphyxiated, their state of unconsciousness rendered them completely unaware of their fate as their body slowly died. Marwood's method of hanging calculated for the individual persons height, weight and their physical condition, all of which determined the correct length of drop required to break that particular persons neck and end their lives in the most efficient and humane manner possible. Although death was generally regarded as being instantaneous, it was not uncommon for the prisoner's heart to take between 15 and 20 minutes to stop beating entirely, when the prison doctor could finally declare them officially dead. Once their death had been pronounced it was then the usual practice in Britain to allow the prisoner's body to hang for an hour before it was finally removed from the gallows and an autopsy carried out.

His successor, James Berry a former policeman, followed Marwood's method of executing condemned prisoners and has been credited with refining his predecessor's calculations into a standardised table of "drops" which were used and improved upon from his time onwards. Although it proved to be a far more reliable method of executing prisoners, mistakes were still known to have occurred, several of which where Berry himself was the hangman. In the one and only instance of the event happening in modern times, Berry as executioner was reported to have miscalculated the length of drop required for a prisoner, which resulted in the condemned man being decapitated by the force of the fall. Two further men nearly suffered the same fate, but their underlying physique just about managed to keep the body intact, much to Berry's obvious relief. In at least one of these instances Berry was quick to point the finger of blame at a Prison Doctor, who he accused of interfering with the length of the rope and thereby causing the near disaster.

However, this wouldn't have accounted for the three prisoners who Berry was accused of giving too short a drop, which was said to have resulted in their slowly being strangled to death and being totally aware of their lives inevitably ebbing away. Far from such instances indicating a problem or failure with the judicial execution process itself, some historians have suggested that these few occurrences point to a fault with Berry himself, rather than the procedure or equipment.

A later executioner, John Ellis, a mild mannered barber from Rochdale in Lancashire followed members of the famous Billington family, who like their later successors, the Pierrepoints, made the execution of condemned prisoners a family business. Ellis was employed in the task from 1901 to 1924 and like the Pierrepoints took his responsibilities and duties as the official executioner extremely seriously, seeking to despatch the condemned prisoner in the most humane and painless way possible.

Unlike many of the other individuals who performed this onerous task however, Ellis seems to have been highly unfortunate when dealing with female prisoners that he was called upon to execute. On the 9th January 1923 he was assigned to execute 28-year-old Edith Jessie Thompson who had been found guilty, along with her paramour Freddie Bywaters, of murdering her husband Percy. The distraught woman had to be physically carried to the gallows by Prison Officers and following her execution her underwear was found to be drenched with her own blood. It was a shocking and distressing discovery for all of those involved, which ultimately led to all future condemned female prisoners having to wear canvas underpants, to prevent a repetition of such an awful occurrence.

Later the same year, Ellis was called upon to execute Susan Newell, the mother of a young girl who had been convicted of killing a teenage newspaper boy in Scotland. Perhaps nervous about hanging yet another woman prisoner, it was reported that Ellis failed to pinion Newell's hands properly, so as he placed the white hood over her head as she stood on the gallows, she was said to have reached up and removed the hood, instructing Ellis "Don't put that on me". Possibly unnerved by this unexpected outburst and action, Ellis was said to have carried on with his duties anyway and launched the highly irascible woman into eternity, with her head and face uncovered.

The third incident which came Ellis' way was at the double execution of Emily Swann and her boyfriend John Gallager, at Armley Jail on 29th December 1903, following their conviction for the murder of Emily's husband William Swann. As she was led into the execution room by Ellis who was assisting William Billington, Emily noticed her lover, already hooded and pinioned on the gallows, "Good morning John" she said to him. Rather startled at the sound of Emily's voice, Gallagher managed to reply "Good morning love". As Ellis placed the noose around Emily's neck she called out "Goodbye love, God bless" at which point Billington pulled the lever, plunging them both to their instantaneous deaths.

Although he would continue with his executioners work for another year, it seems clear that these events and the failing state of his barber's business caused Ellis great emotional and financial hardship, to the point that he finally resigned his position in 1924. However, leaving his post does not seem to have exorcised whatever ghosts or demons that pursued him for the remainder of his life, which only ended with him committing suicide on the 20th September 1932.

Around the same time that John Ellis began his career as an official executioner, Henry Pierrepoint, brother of Thomas and father of the much more notable Albert, began his own career as a hangman. Taking part in over 100 executions, both as principal and assistant, he was noted for the great pride and care that he took in his work, a trait that would be followed by all three members of the family whose name would ultimately became synonymous with the job of official executioner.

Henry's career was cut short however, when in later years he began to drink heavily, although the reason for this has never been fully explained. Needless to say though, such a dependency was always likely to cause problems, which it inevitably did in 1910. Called to an execution at Chelmsford in that year, Henry was reported to have turned up at the jail "worse for wear" the night before the hanging. His assistant was John Ellis, who was said to be an inoffensive sort of man that very few people could find fault with. Perhaps because Ellis had suggested that Henry shouldn't make a habit of drinking before an execution, Henry was reported to have attacked his assistant and knocked him to the floor. A Prison Officer who had heard the commotion rushed into the cell and separated the two men, but not before Henry had struck Ellis for a second time.

The following morning the two men completed the execution of the condemned prisoner in their usually efficient fashion, but the events of the previous evening were reported to the Home Office and a decision was made to strike Henry's name from the official list of executioners. Although he appealed the decision, as far as the authorities were concerned his drinking made him a completely unsuitable person to perform such a responsible and dignified role. It was later reported that Henry had got angry with Ellis because he believed his assistant was trying to replace him as Britain's number one executioner.

During his tenure, Henry was thought to have only participated in the execution of three female prisoners; firstly when he assisted William Billington in the double hanging of Amelia Sachs and Annie Walters at Holloway Prison on December 3rd 1903, both women having been convicted of child murder. His third female execution was that of Rhoda Willis, another "Baby Farmer" who was hung at Cardiff Prison in 1907, with Henry assisted by his brother Thomas. Henry was said to have been particularly struck by the attractive Willis, but whether or not he was adversely affected by having to execute the pretty 44-year-old is unclear.

Thomas Pierrepoint, brother of Henry and uncle to Albert, served as an official executioner between 1906 and 1946 and in common with his relatives was known to have adopted a highly professional and skilful approach to his duties. He was particularly notable for having officiated at the executions of around 16 American servicemen who were convicted of various murders and rapes while they were stationed in Britain during World War II. He is also thought to have been involved with at least four female executions during his time on the list; assisting Henry with the execution of Rhoda Willis in 1907; being the hangman for Louie Calvert at Manchester Strangeways in 1926; executing Dorothea Waddingham at Winsom Green Prison in 1936, where he was said to have assisted by Albert; finally he was the man who executed Charlotte Bryant at Exeter Prison in the same year.

Albert Pierrepoint was reputed to be the most prolific official British executioner of the 20th century and has been credited with executing over 400 men and 17 women during his time in the post, from 1932 through to 1956. Although it has been reported that he executed around 600 people during his career, this number might be accounted for by the inclusion of 200 Nazi war criminals that he was called upon to execute following the end of World War II, ten of which were women.

It was Albert who executed the final woman to be condemned to death in 1955. 28-year-old Ruth Ellis who had been convicted of murdering her lover David Blakely, was hung at Holloway Prison on 13th July in that year amidst a blaze of negative publicity, some of which was aimed at Pierrepoint himself.. Despite rumours to the contrary, Pierrepoint never expressed any regrets over Ruth Ellis' death personally; and his later statements about the rights and wrongs of capital punishment have largely been dismissed as publicity for his own later autobiography, rather than anything else.

Any suggestion however, that the campaign for the abolition of the death penalty was entirely gender driven is incorrect. British criminal history is littered with numerous female killers who were just as naive, jealous, greedy and cruel, as any of their male counterparts and in some cases much more so. Although it is sometimes difficult to understand how a woman, with her inborn maternal and nurturing instincts can deliberately take the life of a young child, poison her husband or cold-bloodedly beat another person to death for no good reason, clearly they can, because they have.

Victorian "Baby Farmers" that deliberately killed young children and babies in their care, in order to gain a relatively small sum of money were almost entirely women, although no doubt there were a small number of men involved in these unscrupulous practices. The fact that poison is and was seen as a woman's "weapon" tends to indicate a preference for this method of killing by a number of female murderers, being an act that required little physical strength to achieve. A lack of physical prowess though has not precluded women from killing others by violent means, they are just as adept at beating, stabbing and shooting other people to death, as is any man, but often such actions are purely the result of a violent emotional outburst, or a temporary loss of control, possibly caused by drink or drugs. However, in the case of the ten Nazi female war criminals that were executed by the British after World War II, there seems to have been some sort of collective or group madness accounting for their often brutal behaviour, rather than any sort of individual plan or choice on the part of the offenders themselves.

Many people regard Ruth Ellis' execution as a "watershed" in the debate over the rights and wrongs of Capital Punishment, although executions continued for another nine years when two convicted male killers were simultaneously executed at Manchester Strangeways and Liverpool's Walton in 1964. The death of a pretty 28-year-old mother, who committed what many regarded as a "crime of passion" gave impetus to an abolitionist campaign that had been simmering for some time and they used her case, along with others, to call for a complete cessation of the practice.

It is perhaps worth pointing out with regard to Ruth Ellis, that it was she who fundamentally and deliberately condemned herself by plainly stating at her trial that she intended to kill her victim, which left the judge with little option but to sentence her to death. There is a sense with the Ellis case particularly, that she had purposefully decided that if she couldn't have Blakely, then no-one else would be able to and she was quite content to pay the price for her act of violence which ultimately brought his life to an end.

Opponents of judicial executions pointed to evidence which suggested that even in countries where capital punishment had been abolished there had been no discernible increase in the numbers of murders, indicating that in itself a death penalty was not a deterrent to those who intended to kill another person.

They also claimed that the prospect or the very idea of a person fighting for their life on the gallows would engender a level of sympathy for the condemned, rather than for the murder victim and that it would inevitably lead to intrusive and morbid investigations by the media, who were looking for a good story. They also pointed out that the death sentence was by its very nature irrevocable and that innocent people might end up paying the ultimate price for a crime they did not commit, which was known to have happened in a number of instances.

Finally, the same opponents claimed that the state by refusing to take a life was in fact strengthening the sanctity of life, presumably making it less likely for an individual to take the life of his fellow citizen. It was also claimed that it was the Christian duty of any modern society to try and redeem the offender, rather than to simply execute them.

Whatever, the rights and wrongs, pros or cons, of the abolitionist arguments, in 1965 the British Government of the time substantially removed the death penalty from the statute book and subsequent political leaderships have essentially prevented any chance of it being reinstated.

The 27 cases that follow are not intended to be wholly definitive records on the women themselves, nor a review of their individual cases from a particular standpoint, but simply offer an overview of their lives, their crimes and ultimately their deaths at the hands of the British state. Each one of these women was a unique individual, but often their crimes were purely the result of basic human frailties, including greed, jealousy and a loss of basic reasoning, which allowed them to ignore both the social conventions and criminal penalties of the time and commit such heinous crimes that they too would ultimately be robbed of their own lives on the state's gallows.

2. A TRULY MYSTERIOUS MURDER

LOUISE JOSEPHINE MASSET

Convicted of murdering 4 year old Manfred Masset

Born around 1864, Louise Josephine Masset was the second daughter of Etienne Ernest Masset and his wife Elizabeth, whose maiden name was Refell. Louise was reported to have lived and worked in France during the second half of the 19th century and as the result of a love affair with a Frenchman was said to have found herself pregnant with his child around 1896. Despite her own apparent disregard of social conventions, she soon realised that being an unmarried mother, alone and abroad, would inevitably put her and the child in very difficult circumstances and so she decided to return home to England, to be close to her family and friends.

Having delivered a baby boy, Manfred Louis, on the 24th April 1896, Louise was said to have settled down to a new life in England, but not before she had made arrangements for her new baby to be placed with a nurse-cum-foster mother, Helen Gentle, who lived in the Tottenham area of London. The cost of caring for the young Manfred was reported to have been met by his father, who had remained in France, but obviously took his obligations to the boy very seriously.

As for Louise herself, she was said to have settled down to live with her sister Leonie and her brother-in-law Richard Cadisch at Bethune Road, Stoke Newington and found employment as a private day governess and part-time piano teacher. At least once a week though, it was said that she would go to see her son, spend a few hours with him and according to Helen Gentle behave as any mother in her circumstances would.

The road to Louise' ultimate ruin and the death of young Manfred was thought to have begun when she started a friendship with a young French bank clerk, Eudore Lucas, who was a neighbour of Louise's sister Leonie; and at 19 years of age was at least 15 years younger than Louise herself. Lucas was in England ostensibly to gain experience in his chosen profession of finance and as a junior clerk was thought to be paid very little money, which has been one suggested reason for the horrendous events that were to take place in the final few months of 1899.

On the 16th October of that year, Louise was said to have contacted Helen Gentle and informed her that Manfred's father had expressed the wish to have his son live with him in France and advised her that she would collect the child on Friday 27th October 1899. Although she was a little surprised at the sudden announcement and perhaps a little sad that Manfred would be leaving her, Mrs Gentle does not appear to have any serious reservations about the change of circumstance and happily agreed to meet Louise to deliver the boy to her.

Eleven days later and at the appointed time, the two women met at Stamford Hill, where after a tearful farewell Manfred was handed over to his mother, along with his favourite toy and a parcel of clothes that his foster mother had prepared for him. As Helen Gentle made her way home, she could not have imagined that within the space of a few hours her former charge would be viciously beaten and suffocated by the woman she had just freely handed him over to; and that the next time she would see him, he would be lying lifeless on a mortuary slab.

Having departed Stamford Hill with the tearful young Manfred in her care, Louise was first thought to have made her way to London Bridge railway station, where they were reported to have been seen in a first-class waiting room at about 1.45 pm. Around three o'clock the same afternoon, a female attendant, a Mrs Rees, noticed the couple and remembered later that the young boy appeared to be distressed. When she commented to the woman about the child's apparent unhappiness, the woman replied that he might be hungry and that she would take him for something to eat at a nearby shop. With that, the woman collected the young boy and her belongings, left the waiting room and set off in the direction of a nearby store. Some three hours later the same woman, later identified as Louise, was seen once again by Mrs Rees at London Bridge railway station, but this time without the child and was seen to be hurriedly making her way to catch the six o'clock Brighton train.

Around twenty minutes later, at the nearby Dalston Junction railway station, two female passengers, Mary Teahan and Margaret Biggs, entered the ladies waiting room and were horrified to discover the naked body of a young boy, partially covered by a black shawl. The Police and a doctor having been called to the scene, it soon emerged that the child had in fact been beaten unconscious with a brick which lay nearby and subsequently smothered, probably by the murderers hand being clamped over his nose and mouth. Within days, the grim discovery had been headlined in all of the major newspapers, so it wasn't long before potential witnesses came forward to help the Police with their murder enquiry.

One of the people who read the gruesome story was Helen Gentle, Manfred Masset's foster mother who had earlier handed her young charge over to his mother Louise. However, within days of the child leaving her care, she had received a letter from Louise Masset telling her that Manfred was missing her dreadfully, but that he was well and would undoubtedly settle into his new home over time. Mrs Gentle remained troubled however and believed that the body found at Dalston Junction may well be that of young Manfred, a belief that was soon confirmed after she contacted the Police and was asked to view the dead child's body. By this time, the Police had also recovered items of Manfred's clothing which had been left at Brighton railway station and the foster mother was able to identify those as having belonged to the murdered boy. This identification had been made easier by the fact that Helen Gentle had taken a final photograph of young Manfred on the day that he was taken away by his mother and helped to positively identify both him and his clothing beyond any reasonable doubt.

With the murdered boy's identity confirmed and armed with the information provided by Helen Gentle, the Police were now seeking his mother as their main suspect in the crime and it wasn't long before they apprehended her at the home of a second sister, who lived with her husband George Symes in Streatham Road in Croydon.

Asked to account for her whereabouts and the murder of her young child, Louise was reported to have invented a story which laid the blame on two mysterious women called Browning. According to her, she had met and become friendly with the two women, who told her that they operated a boarding school of sorts in Chelsea and that young Manfred would benefit greatly from being enrolled there. Louise claimed that on the day that she took Manfred from Helen Gentle, she had then met with the two women and had paid them a sum of money for her son's care and simply handed him over to these two strangers. Her belief was that these two women were entirely to blame for her child's death and although she may have been negligent in passing her son to them, she was totally innocent of killing him. When pressed by the Police however, to offer more information or proof of this supposed transaction and the two mystery women named Browning, she was unable to provide any evidence to support her claim, not even a receipt for the money that she was said to have paid them for his care.

In the meantime, the evidence implicating Louise in the crime continued to mount, with the Police continuing to make enquiries at both Dalston Junction railway station and London Bridge station, as well as the surrounding areas. Mrs Rees, the female waiting room attendant who had seen the woman and child at London Bridge station came forward and identified Louise as the woman in question. The Police were also helped by a shop assistant in Stoke Newington who was able to identify the black shawl which had partially covered young Manfred's naked body as being one that they had sold two days before the killing. They remembered it had been purchased by a woman with a French sounding accent, a peculiarity of Louise who had not only lived in France but was half French on her father's side.

When asked by the Police to account for her movements over the weekend when Manfred was killed, Louise freely admitted that she had travelled to Brighton to spend a few days in a hotel with her young French paramour, Eudore Lucas. The damning fact that some of Manfred's clothes had been left at Brighton railway station was bad enough, but then a young chambermaid from the hotel in question informed the authorities that she had recovered the boy's favourite toy from the room in which Louise and Eudore had stayed over that terrible weekend.

With the overwhelming weight of evidence against her the Police charged Louise with the murder of her son Manfred Louis Masset and she stood trial at the Old Bailey in the middle of December 1899 before Mr Justice Bruce. Her highly questionable defence involving the probably fictional Browning women was quickly dismissed and she was found guilty by a jury of her peers. Throughout her trial, which saw a procession of witnesses testify against her, Louise was reported to have remained calm, almost aloof from the proceedings. It was only when Mr Justice Bruce pronounced the death sentence on her did she show any sort of emotion and then she was reported to have collapsed in the dock, only to be revived to hear the full and deadly sentence levied against her.

After sentencing she was held at the capital's fearsome Newgate Prison where the punishment was to be carried out. She was held in the condemned cell over the Christmas period of 1899 and on into the dawn of the 20th Century, thereby guaranteeing her immortality as the first female prisoner executed in that new century. Shortly before her death it was said that she had confessed to murdering her child, but there appears to no record available, as to why she committed such a terrible act.

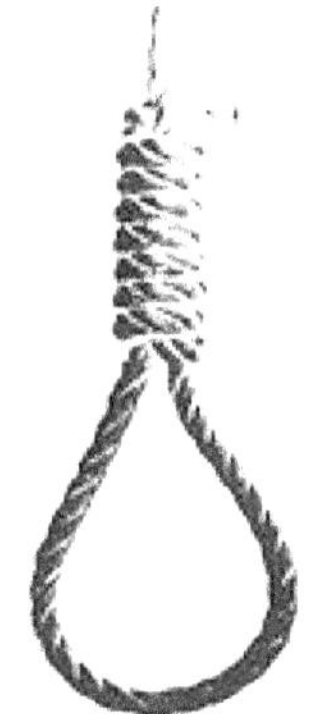

Some correspondents have interpreted her admission, "The sentence was just", as being simply a rebuke or condemnation to herself, for supposedly passing her only child to the mysterious "Browning" women who subsequently murdered the young boy. However, it seems highly unlikely that a woman who was facing her end and possibly her creator would be so enigmatic, if she truly believed that someone else had been responsible for Manfred's death. Rather, it seems much more likely that Louise simply couldn't bring herself to say the words "I am guilty" and instead chose another way to admit her liability.

Pleas for clemency were made on her behalf, including one by her brother-in-law, citing widespread insanity within the family lines, but ultimately they were all rejected or simply ignored. Consequently, at exactly nine o'clock on 9th January 1900, the executioner James Billington stepped into the condemned cell at Newgate Prison and without a word, placed a leather belt around her waist and pinioned her arms to her sides. She was then led across the prison yard to the execution shed on the far side and once inside was placed on the gallows trapdoor. Her legs were then pinioned beneath her long skirts and the noose was placed around her neck, before Billington placed the white hood over her head, released the retaining pin and pulled the lever which launched her into the void below. After her body had hung on the gallows for the customary hour, Louise' remains were finally taken down and placed in a simple wooden coffin, ready for burial within the prisons precincts.

3. THE BATTERSEA BABY KILLER

ADA CHARD WILLIAMS

Convicted of murdering a 21-month-old baby girl Selina Ellen Jones

Perhaps because no mother would willingly hand her child over to a male stranger, the common Victorian practice of "baby farming" was almost entirely a female venture or occupation that was perpetrated against members of their own gender and the most vulnerable of victims; children. At a time when contraception was as much a case of luck, as any sort of planning, it was not unusual to find large numbers of young unmarried women looking for solutions to their unexpected pregnancies and what to do with the babies, which were generally unexpected and unaffordable.

Florence Jones found herself in this predicament towards the end of 1897, when as the result of a relationship she delivered a baby girl called Selina Ellen in December of that year. Florence was not married to Selina's father and still lived at home with her parents in Croydon, but with financial help from her partner she arranged for the baby to be fostered out with a Mrs Muller for the first three months of her life, during which time she was said to have thrived.

She would later testify that she had removed Selina from Mrs Muller because of concerns over the baby's health and re-housed her with a Mrs Wetherall at a cost of five shillings a week and this was where the baby remained until the end of August 1899. Sometime during this period Selina's father was thought to have stopped paying towards her keep and the weekly amount paid to Mrs Wetherall was reduced to half-a-crown per week, although this obviously did not affect her care of the child.

Although Florence seems to have been entirely happy with the care offered by the foster mother, this did not stop her noticing an advert placed in the Woolwich Herald in August 1899, which stated that a young married couple would like to adopt a healthy young baby provided that certain terms were met. She subsequently contacted a Mrs Hewetson from Hammersmith who had placed the advert, enclosing a photograph of Selina and requesting that she provide full details of the arrangement and terms required. Within days she had received a reply from the advertiser, stating that she and her husband would like to adopt Selina, they required a fee of £5 and would like to meet her personally to discuss the matter more fully.

On the 24th August 1899, Florence met Mrs Hewetson at Woolwich railway station to discuss the matter of a possible adoption. The two women visited Florence's mother in Croydon and it was agreed that Selina would stay with the Hewetson's for a while, but would ultimately be returned to her family and that both Florence and her mother would visit Selina from time to time, all of which was agreed to by Mrs Hewetson. Before they parted, Florence told Hewetson that she would bring Selina to their next meeting, in a week's time, that she would hand the child over then and pay her three of the five pounds that they had agreed for Selina's costs.

Seemingly happy that she had made a good decision for her daughter's care, Florence later contacted Mrs Wetherall and told her that she had made new arrangements for Selina and that she would collect her on the following Thursday, the 31st August. In the days prior to this date, Florence was reported to have bought some new clothes for her daughter, as a gift for her new foster parents, including a new plaid dress, which would later become a significant item in the subsequent murder trial.

On Thursday 31st August 1899 Florence arrived at Mrs Wetherall's home to collect her daughter and after a tearful farewell she left with the 21-month-old, along with a bundle of clothes and proceeded to her meeting with Mrs Hewetson at Charing Cross Station. The two women having met, they then travelled to Hammersmith where Florence was shown the Hewetson's new house there, but wasn't able to go inside the property as a group of workmen were busily renovating it. They then walked to the home of one of Mrs Hewetson's friends, Mrs Woolmer, where they took tea and settled the matter of the £3 down-payment which had previously been agreed between the two women.

With their business concluded, the two women and Selina walked back to Hammersmith station where Florence took her leave of Mrs Hewetson and her daughter and made her way back to her parent's home in Croydon. On parting, they had agreed that Mrs Hewetson would contact Florence in a day or so, in order that she could settle the balance of the money owed to the couple, but not having heard from them after a few days she became increasingly worried about her young daughter.

On Sunday 3rd September 1899, Florence travelled to Hammersmith and immediately went to the house that Mrs Hewetson had identified as her home. Having knocked on the door however, it soon became clear that the family within the house did not know anyone called Hewetson and had no knowledge of her daughter Selina. Florence then walked to the local newsagents, that was owned by a Mr Canning and asked about Mrs Hewetson, but he was unable to offer any information that would help to locate the mysterious woman. It later transpired that his shop was being used as a "mail box" by a number of different people, who paid a penny for every letter delivered there and who would simply turn up and collect the letters on a regular basis.

Florence then made her way to the home of Mrs Woolmer, the "friend" of Mrs Hewetson, who told her that Hewetson had in fact simply rented a room from her, but had subsequently left the property and had left no forwarding address. It now began to dawn on Florence that all was not as it seemed and having returned to her parents to inform them of the circumstances, she then contacted the Police and made a formal complaint.

It didn't take long for the Police to follow up Florence Jones' own enquiries, at the house in Hammersmith, Mr Canning's newsagents shop and the home of the entirely innocent Mrs Woolmer. They soon learned that Mrs Hewetson was in fact a woman called Ada Chard Williams, who was married to a school teacher called William Chard Williams, both of whom had seemingly disappeared from the area. With very little information to go on and given the itinerant nature of the two suspects, the Police soon ran out of leads in their investigation and it became temporarily stalled, leaving Florence uncertain as to her young daughter's ultimate fate.

On the 27th September 1899, a bargeman called William Stokes who was working on the River Thames near Battersea made a grim discovery that would ultimately confirm Florence Jones' worst suspicions, when he spotted a parcel that seemed to contain the body of a child. Calling to a Police Officer named Voice who was patrolling nearby, he identified the package and the constable retrieved it from the waters edge, immediately noting that a young child's foot was sticking out of the tightly bound parcel.

PC Voice accompanied the body to the local mortuary at Battersea and was involved in unwrapping and untying the tightly bound remains, observing that the body was that of a young girl who had been wrapped in flannelette, wore a napkin around her lower portions and had her head covered with a white bag. Around her neck was a length of material, similar to the bag and her limbs had been tied with pieces of window sash cord and string. As a former naval man, Voice also noticed that both the cord and string contained a number of different knots including reef, half-hitch and the less usual fisherman's bend, a discovery which would ultimately prove to be significant.

Once the body had been unwrapped and untied, the Divisional Police Surgeon Doctor Kempster was able to perform an autopsy on the young girl and determined that she had died from being suffocated, having first been beaten unconscious by her attacker. Although it was later suggested that she might have been drowned by being placed in the river, the surgeon was confident that his findings were correct and the girl had been strangled or suffocated before being placed in the water. It also became clear from his examination that despite some level of decomposition, the body might well have been in the water for a relatively short time, suggesting that the girl might only have been killed fairly recently.

The following day, Florence Jones was asked to attend the mortuary and quickly identified the body of her missing daughter. Although she was the mother of the child, the Police also requested that Martha Wetherall, Selina's former carer, should make a formal identification of the remains which she did, pointing out a small scar on the child's face that she herself had accidentally caused.

With this painful part of the investigation completed, the Police were now seeking two murder suspects and it was Ada Chard Williams herself that would initiate the next phase of the inquiry. The capital's newspapers all carried details of the gruesome case and it was as a result of their headlines that Williams became aware that the body of young Selina Jones had in fact been recovered. Keen to distance herself from any sort of responsibility in the murder, she wrote to the Police admitting her part as a baby farmer, but claiming that she had handed the child over to another woman called Smith who lived in the Croydon area and that she herself had played no part in the young girl's death.

However, her act of contacting the Police to declare her innocence soon led them to her door and on December 8th 1899 both she and her husband were arrested and charged at their home in Gainsborough Road, Hackney by Detective Inspector Scott and Sergeant Gough. With the couple in custody a search of their house and belongings was made by officers and a large number of child's clothes were found at the Gainsborough Road property. It has also been claimed, that during their search the Police discovered a number of packages that were bound with string and found to contain the highly unusual fisherman's bend knot that had been found on the restraints holding the dead girl's body.

A month earlier in November 1899, Detective Inspector Scott, accompanied by Sergeant Windsor had visited the Williams' former home at Grove Villas, Grove Road in Barnes and found the property empty but for some window cord and string, similar to those that had been used to bind Selina's body and the wrappings used to cover her lifeless form. As part of their investigation, the officers had spoken to Mr and Mrs Loughborough who lived at No. 2 Grove Villas, who informed them that Ada and William Chard Williams had been their neighbours, living at No. 3 Grove Villas until around October 1899.

More significantly, Mrs Loughborough remembered that initially the Williams' had lived at No. 3 with a baby boy called Freddy, who she thought was around 10-months-old and was the only child in the house up until August of that year. In the first week of September however, a young girl arrived at the house, who Mrs Loughborough considered to be around 2-years-old. Ada Williams had told her that the little girl was called Lily and that she was her sister's daughter who lived in Uxbridge.

The witness also told Police about Mrs Williams' apparent cruelty to the child, having seen her slap the girl for no obvious reason and related how Williams was reported to have beaten her with a stick because she was unfortunate enough to have soiled herself. It also became apparent from her evidence, that William Chard Williams, the husband, appeared to be completely dominated by his wife, but tried to be kind and to defend the young girl that had recently arrived in their house.

A couple of days after Ada Williams was reported to have beaten young Lily, Mrs Loughborough told how she had called round to No. 3 Grove Villas and had actually seen the weal's on the young girls back which were dark red in colour. She remembered asking herself how any woman could leave their child with someone like Williams. Her memory of the girl called Lily was that she was thin and never seemed to be allowed in the garden, taken out for exercise and always seemed to be crying.

Over the weekend of the 25th September 1899, Mrs Loughborough and her family went away to visit relatives at Greenwich and only returned on the following Monday. Having arrived back, she was immediately struck by the lack of noise from No. 3 and when she asked Ada Chard Williams about Lily was simply told that the little girl had gone home to her mother. Around the same time Williams was also said to have offered an exchange to Mrs Loughborough, swapping some clothes Lily's mother had left behind for a flower pot that Williams had seen in the Loughborough house. The items of clothing given to her by Chard Williams included; two flannel petticoats, pink socks, vests, drawers and more significantly a plaid frock, all of which were later handed to Detective Inspector Scott and were subsequently identified by Florence Jones as having belonged to her daughter Selina.

With the mass of evidence laid against them, both Ada and William Chard Williams were indicted for the murder of Selina Ellen Jones and stood trial at the Old Bailey between the 16th and 17th December 1899 before Mr Justice Ridley. After two days of almost irrefutable prosecution evidence, countered only be the habitual excuse of a fictional third party being involved in the girl's death, it only took the jury a little time to convict Ada Chard Williams of murder. Her hapless husband was far more fortunate than his spouse, the jury choosing to believe that in all probability he played no part in killing the helpless toddler. He was however convicted of assisting and harbouring Ada Chard Williams who had committed murder, but at least escaped with his life.

On the morning of Wednesday 8th March 1900 James Billington entered the condemned cell at Newgate Prison, the last time any British executioner would do so and quickly pinioned Ada Chard Williams' arms to her side. He then led her along the same route that some eight weeks before Louise Masset had walked, across the prison yard to the execution shed which stood across the way. Placing her on the trapdoor of the gallows, Billington quickly strapped her legs beneath her long skirt, placed the rope expertly around her neck and placed the white hood over her head. With all completed, he then stepped back, released the holding pin and pulled the lever which sent her plummeting into the space below and causing her neck to dislocate instantly.

Although the 24-year-old was tried and convicted of only one murder, there were suspicions that she was likely to have committed many more in her career as a baby farmer, all of which remained unsolved or simply unreported. Whatever the merits of those suspicions however, the fact that she lost her life for a measly three pounds, albeit a decent sum at the time, is testimony to the greed and foolishness of those women who chose to pursue such a career path. Her only contribution to society is to be remembered as the final woman to be hanged at Newgate Prison, before such practices were finally removed to the new penitentiary at Holloway, a truly miserable epitaph for any woman.

4. THE CLONBROCK MURDER

MARY DALY

Convicted of murdering her husband John Daly

Reported to have been born in 1865 to James Byrne and his wife Mary, of Queens County in Ireland, Mary Daly was one of nine children, having four brothers and four sisters. She was said to have married her husband John Daly in 1890 and fairly quickly delivered him two children, a son called John and a daughter called Elizabeth.

The family were said to have lived on a modest smallholding within Queens County, although John was known to be gainfully employed as a carrier, transporting and selling materials from a nearby quarry to customers within the wider region. It was long and tiring work, which often necessitated him being away from home for days at a time and it was perhaps these enforced absences that directly led to his wife forming an unfortunate attachment with a younger man that would have such tragic consequences for all three people.

Although there is little direct evidence that John Daly was either an indolent or abusive husband, it may well be that his work related absences from home caused a degree of frustration or loneliness for his wife, who was not only tied to the family farm but was left with the responsibility of raising their two young children unaided. It was perhaps little wonder then, that when a neighbour's son who was ten years her junior came into her rather mundane life, that she found her head turned and her feelings towards her husband changed.

The adulterous relationship between Mary and her young paramour, Joseph Taylor, soon became the subject for the local gossips, but whether her husband John was actually aware of the affair is unclear. It is known however, that the relationship between Mary and her young lover must have been fairly tempestuous, as in May 1902 it was reported that Joseph had visited the Daly house and attacked Mary, striking her with an axe. The assault was considered to be serious enough that the Police became involved and Taylor was arrested for the attack, charged and brought before the courts. On the day of the trial however, it was recorded that Mary Daly failed to attend to give evidence against Taylor, so the authorities had little choice but to release him. Whether on not Taylor was a naturally aggressive individual isn't known, but given the reported attack on Mary and the subsequent events which led to the death of John Daly, it seems clear that he did indeed have a propensity for violence, although maybe only after drinking heavily.

What Mary's husband, John, actually made of the events involving his wife, isn't known, but it seems reasonable to conclude that their fraught relationship was likely to have degenerated further, given that the state of their marriage would undoubtedly have been discussed by all and sundry. On the 17th June 1902, John Daly was said to have gone about his business as usual, transporting a load from the local quarry to the town of Carlow. Having completed his work, he was then thought to have headed home and upon reaching the farm, would normally have unhitched his horse, before releasing it into the small paddock at the rear of the property.

The following morning however, his wife Mary was said to have noticed that he had not come to bed, but that both horse and cart were in their usual places. Calling her son, John, she asked him to look around for his father and within minutes the boy had returned to tell her, that his father was lying in the field at the back of the house. Going into the paddock to confirm the boy's story, she then found the body of her husband lying dead on the ground, with the horses bridle still grasped in his hand and his head resting in a pool of his own blood.

Mary quickly sent 11-year-old John to fetch the Police, reminding him to relate the events as he was told by her, that she had retired to bed around eleven o'clock the previous evening, had not been disturbed by her husbands return and had woken the following morning to find the horse and cart returned, but no obvious sign of her husband, until young John had discovered his body in the field.

Sometime later, the Police arrived at the farm and immediately set about surveying the murder scene. It soon became clear that John Daley had suffered a prolonged and vicious attack, during which he had been stabbed several times around the head, sustained a serious wound to the side of his face and had ultimately bled out and died. The officers also noticed, that in addition to the pool of blood beneath the victims head, there was a second one some yards away and a broken section of a garden fork which was covered with blood. Upon further investigation, the missing piece of the fork was found lying close to a stream which lay across the paddock, somewhere in between the Daly's farm and that of their neighbours, the home of Joseph Taylor.

Having collected all of the evidence and spoken to all of the relevant witnesses, the Police quickly came to the conclusion that they had sufficient circumstantial evidence to arrest Joseph Taylor for the murder of John Daly, which they did on 19th June 1902. Within a matter of days, Taylor was said to have implicated his lover, Mary Daly, in the murder of her husband and on Tuesday the 24th June 1902, Police arrived at the family farm to arrest her for conspiracy to murder. Both parties were now formally charged with involvement in the death of John Daly and were remanded into custody.

At the Leinster Winter Assizes, held at Mayborough on Friday 12th December 1902 they were brought to trial, where both Daly and Taylor pleaded "Not Guilty" to the charges laid against them. After some legal argument it was agreed by the court that Mary Daly should be tried separately and she was remanded to stand trial alone on Wednesday 18th December 1902.

Despite his assertions of being innocent of the charges laid against him, Taylor had in fact condemned himself, in the statements that he had made to the Police regarding his accomplice Mary Daly. He told them that she had tried on a number of occasions to persuade him to kill her husband, in one instance even suggesting poison as a method of killing him, but Taylor refused saying that he would not have been a party to such an act. However, the fact that he had not informed the authorities of her intentions and the very fact that her husband had eventually turned up dead, made his protests of innocence look very doubtful.

The appearance in the witness box of young John Daly, the dead man's son, who was called as one of the prosecutions main witnesses, effectively negated any possible defence by Taylor, even when his barrister tried to disparage and undermine the young boy's evidence.

Eleven-year-old John Daly Junior told the court that on the night of the murder Taylor had visited their home and had been engaged in whispered conversations with his mother. He and his sister Elizabeth had been sent to bed at around 9.30 pm and had been woken some hours later by the sound of shouting in the yard below. Both he and Elizabeth had got out of bed to investigate the noise and having gone downstairs, found Joseph Taylor attacking their father who was lying on the floor, pleading for mercy. The young witness told the court that Taylor then dragged their father over the stile leading to the paddock at the rear of the house and the next thing they heard was the noise of the garden fork being beaten against something.

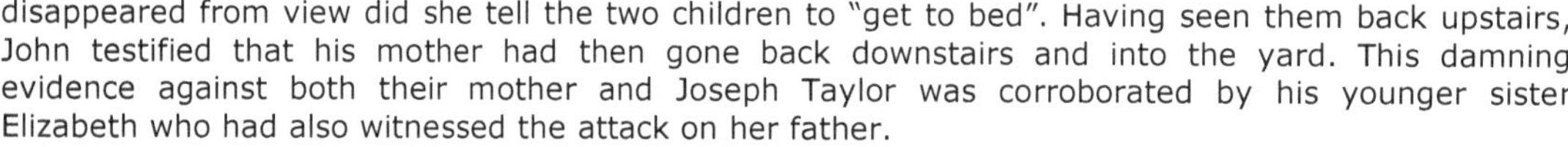

When asked what his mother had been doing during the altercation, John told the court that she had just watched as Taylor beat their father and only after the two men had disappeared from view did she tell the two children to "get to bed". Having seen them back upstairs, John testified that his mother had then gone back downstairs and into the yard. This damning evidence against both their mother and Joseph Taylor was corroborated by his younger sister Elizabeth who had also witnessed the attack on her father.

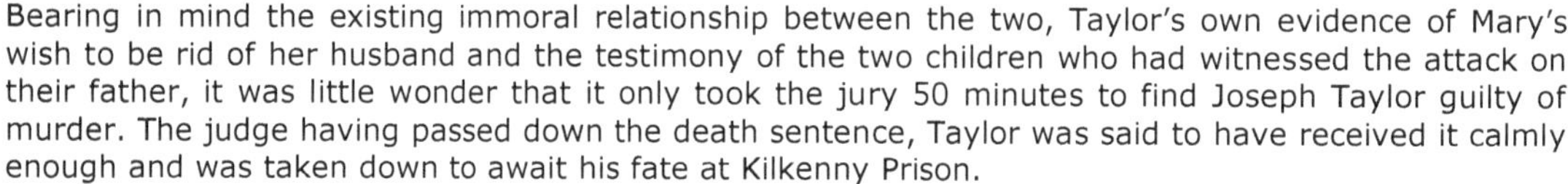

Bearing in mind the existing immoral relationship between the two, Taylor's own evidence of Mary's wish to be rid of her husband and the testimony of the two children who had witnessed the attack on their father, it was little wonder that it only took the jury 50 minutes to find Joseph Taylor guilty of murder. The judge having passed down the death sentence, Taylor was said to have received it calmly enough and was taken down to await his fate at Kilkenny Prison.

Days later, on the 18th December 1902, Mary Daly stood trial for the murder of her husband John, the case being heard before Mr Justice Kenny. Aside from the statements made by her co-accused, about her wish to see her husband dead, the main prosecution witness was once again the defendants own son, John Junior, who repeated his testimony about the night of the murder for the court.

In her defence, Mary told the court that both Taylor and her husband had been drinking heavily and that what started out as a drunken brawl soon developed into a murderous assault which she was powerless to prevent. She claimed to have been as shocked as her two children but had not played a part in her husband's killing, as it was a spontaneous event there could be no question of her having intentionally planned his death.

The Crown however had a different view of her character and her actions on that fateful night. The prosecutor painted a picture of an adulterous wife who had deliberately abandoned her marital vows and was obviously unbowed and indifferent to the fact that her immoral behaviour was the subject of local gossip. He pointed to the statements of Joseph Taylor who had claimed that Mary had implored him on several occasions to do away with her husband, even suggesting that her lover might poison her spouse, so that they might be together.

He then spoke about the night of the murder itself, of Mary's apparent inactivity as her husband was first beaten and then dragged away to be mercilessly stabbed with the garden fork. He pointed to her failure to seek help for her husband, either from the Police or from neighbours, despite the fact that she was free to flee the scene at any time. She had made no effort to render her fatally injured husband with any sort of aid, but instead chose to fabricate a version of the night's events which would draw attention away from herself and her lover, Joseph Taylor. Finally, the prosecutor told the court, she had not only lied herself, but she had also instructed her children to lie to the authorities, a sure indication that she was trying to hide her own complicity in the murder, she may not have struck the fatal blow, but she had surely conspired to ensure that it was delivered.

Within an hour of the jury being sent out to consider their verdict they had returned with one of "Guilty". When she heard the word, Mary Daly was reported to have appeared stunned by their decision, perhaps still believing that she had played no real part in her husband's death. With the verdict given however, it only remained for the judge to deliver the dreaded sentence of death to the disbelieving Daly, after which she was taken down and delivered to Tullamore Prison where she would spend the remaining weeks of her life.

At eight o'clock on the morning of 7th January 1903, William Billington, Britain's official executioner stepped into the condemned cell at Ireland's Kilkenny Prison and quickly pinioned 26-year-old Joseph Taylor's arms, before leading him to the gallows. As he stood on the trapdoor, his legs were strapped, the noose placed around his neck and finally the white hood placed over his head. Stepping back from the prisoner, Billington then released the pin and pulled the lever, dropping Taylor into the void below and instantly dislocating his neck. After the customary hour, his body was taken down and placed in a coffin ready for burial.

Three days later at Tullamore Prison, at eight o'clock in the morning on the 10th January 1903, the same William Billington stepped into the condemned cell there and without delay pinioned Mary Daly's arms, before leading her to the gallows. Her legs were strapped under her long skirt, the noose placed expertly around her neck, before the white hood was finally placed over her head. Stepping back, he released the retaining pin and pulled the lever which immediately despatched the 36-year-old mother of two into the abyss below and bringing an end to a fairly sordid and sorry business.

5. THE FINCHLEY BABY FARMERS

AMELIA SACHS & ANNIE WALTERS

Convicted of murdering a baby surnamed Galley

Crime partnerships in themselves are not that unremarkable, but where both participants are women, their victims are innocent babies and where the perpetrators played a part in the final double female execution in British legal history, then these two women are indeed notable.

The younger of the two, Amelia Sachs, seems to have been the "brains" behind a murderous venture which is claimed to have cost up to twenty new born infants their lives and netted Sachs and her co-conspirator what we would now regard as a fairly paltry sum of money.

Born in 1873, Amelia Sachs was a married woman with a child of her own, who either through design or circumstance had established a business at Claymore House in Finchley, which financially exploited unfortunate young women who found themselves carrying a child out of wedlock, which was a clear breach of the social conventions and etiquette of Victorian England. Setting up what we might now call an unmarried mothers home, Sachs advertised for suitable young women to lodge with her until their babies were delivered and then offered them the possibility of their new born baby being adopted by childless couples or wealthy individuals. For most of her clients, who were generally unable or unwilling to take on the responsibility of an unplanned child, the chance to have their baby adopted by a loving couple or a well-to-do person was an extremely acceptable solution to their presently uncertain predicament.

This was not a purely altruistic gesture on Sachs' part however. Generally, the unmarried mother would be asked for a "present" for the potential parents, a financial sweetener of between £20 and £30 which might be used by the adoptive parents to buy things for their new baby. As most of the young women were keen to give their baby's the very best start in life, they would often ask the infants father for the money required, which in most cases they were more than happy to do, just to see the unexpected problem go away.

What none of these unfortunate young women realised, was that these potential new parents were entirely fictional and in reality the babies were simply taken away by an associate of Sachs, a woman called Annie Walters, who subsequently drugged and asphyxiated the babies before dumping their bodies in the River Thames or in another convenient location, where it would remain undiscovered. They were entirely motivated by greed and had realised early on that by killing the children, they could not only keep the money given to them for the baby's new adoptive parents, but also that they could sell the belongings left for the child by its natural mother.

Annie Walters was reported to have been born in 1869, although other records say she was 54 years old at the time of her death, indicating that she had in fact been born in 1849. She too was married, but was said to have been separated from her husband and there is no information as to her having had children herself. It is known however, that she was semi-illiterate, feeble-minded and had a chronic drinking problem, all of which no doubt accounted for her subservience to the much more calculating and able Amelia Sachs.

The usual method of murdering the new born babies was for Sachs to attend the delivery of the infant and then take it out of the room in order to wash it. Occasionally she would return the baby, so that the mother could say farewell, before she handed it over to Walters who would bundle the baby up and remove it from the house. At some point, she would feed the infant with milk that was laced with Chlorodine, a morphine based sedative, which when given to very young children might asphyxia them, or at least render them unconscious. Where the medication did not kill the child outright, it was thought that Walters would simply suffocate the children by placing her hand over the baby's mouth and nose and preventing it from being able to breathe.

Although there is no definitive evidence as to how long Sachs and Walters had been operating their "baby farming" practice, given the numbers of baby clothes found by Police after the pair had been arrested, there are some suggestions that at least twenty babies had perished as a result of their business and possibly more. Fortunately for other potential victims though, it was the careless actions of Annie Walters that would ultimately lead Police to the pair and bring an end to their murderous careers.

For a reason known only to herself, Walters chose to bring one of the infants home with her, rather than dispose of it immediately. It is interesting to speculate whether or not this change had been brought about for a specific reason, possibly as the result of a young mother changing her mind at the last minute and wanting her baby returned. Perhaps unnerved by this or another incident, Walters obviously made a decision to keep the baby with her for a little while, before employing her usual methods and causing it to die from suffocation. Unfortunately for her, her landlord happened to be a serving Police Officer called Henry Seal, whose suspicions would later have such grave results for her and her accomplice Amelia Sachs.

Having brought the baby into her lodgings, on the pretence that she was caring for it temporarily, it obviously caused a good deal of interest amongst the Seal family, including his wife and children, who were all keen to help Walters with caring for the infant. They all noticed however, that within hours of the baby arriving in the house just how quiet the baby became, something that Walters accounted for by it sleeping a lot as a result of her using Chlorodine to settle it. Mrs Seal, an experienced mother herself, was a little disturbed by this admission, but eventually found herself convinced by Walters's argument that small amounts of the drug were relatively harmless. Despite their best efforts to help with or even see the baby, none of the Seal household were able to confirm for themselves that the baby was well and within a couple of days, Walters was said to have taken the baby away, to be re-homed with its new family.

Had Annie Walters refrained from bringing any more children home with her, then it is unlikely that her dark secret would ever have been discovered. However, sometime later she repeated the mistake and once again turned up with a baby at her lodgings, claiming it to be a baby girl that she had been asked to re-home with a wealthy client. Once again she was loathe for the Seal family to have too much contact with the baby and it was only while she was out of the house that Mrs Seal had an opportunity to take a good look at the baby girl. Needing to change the baby's nappy, she was surprised to discover, that in fact it wasn't a girl, but a baby boy instead. When Walters returned to the house and realised that the baby had been changed, her attitude towards the family was far from appreciative and she quickly isolated the baby boy in her room. Needless to say, her behaviour gave the whole Seal family cause for concern and it was perhaps this incident that finally made Henry Seal take a little more interest in his female lodger.

Later Court records suggest that Officer Seal reported his suspicions to his immediate superior, who detailed a detective to follow Annie Walters as she left her lodgings and to see what she did with the baby. On the morning of her arrest the detective watched as she left the house with a bundle under her arm and followed her to the South Kensington railway station, where she appears to have wandered around fairly aimlessly. After she had entered the female lavatories the detective informed the station master as to his concerns and they both approached the toilets. When confronted by Walters the Policeman quickly identified himself and challenged her to show him what was in the bundle. Realising that she had been caught red-handed Walters claimed that she wasn't guilty of murder, but complied with the detectives request and opened the bundle to reveal the lifeless body of a baby boy, who showed signs of having been suffocated. With his worst suspicions confirmed, the shocked detective arrested Walters on the spot for the murder of the boy, who it would transpire, had been born only a few days earlier to a young woman called Ada Galley.

Having been taken to the local Police station and formally charged, Annie Walters was then questioned by detectives, as a result of which the authorities immediately went to Amelia Sachs' "lying-in" home in Finchley and arrested her as an accomplice to the murder of the Galley child. A Police search of her premises and particularly her own private rooms soon revealed evidence of the scale of the practice undertaken by the pair and witnessed by the numbers of children clothes neatly stored away in her drawers and cupboards. Some of these personal items would later prove to be damning evidence against Sachs and Walters, as they were handmade by the mothers of the new born babies and therefore almost unique and easily identifiable.

As the Police investigation delved deeper into the operation of the "Finchley Baby Farmers", so they managed to contact a large number of the young women who had given their newborn children over for adoption. They also managed to contact a handful of the absentee fathers, some of whom were able to provide identification of those involved, as well as the numbers of the bank notes that had been handed over to Amelia Sachs.

One of the most important witnesses however, was a Doctor Wylie, who had personally delivered Ms Galley's baby and recalled that it was such a difficult birth that he had had to use forceps to bring the young boy into the world. When the boy's body had been found in the possession of Annie Walters it had immediately been sent to the mortuary and when he was called to identify the remains, he stated that he recognised the baby, not least because of the slight bruising on his head, which had been caused by the use of forceps.

The pathologist who examined the child's remains would later testify to the court that death was in all probability caused by manual suffocation, as there was no evidence of the baby having been fed for a good many hours before its death, which precluded the likelihood of Walters having used Chlorodine to end the child's life. Although it had been suggested that the bruising on the boys head might be the result of a blow, his general opinion was that the bruising might indeed have been caused by the use of forceps during a difficult delivery.

Another witness that was interviewed by the Police was an assistant that worked in a Coffee House, who recalled that she remembered Walters being in her establishment, clutching a small child that was wrapped up in a bundle of clothes. She told how she had spoken to Walters and commented on how quiet the baby was, to which she replied, that the child had just come out of hospital and was still under the anaesthetic. The assistant would later testify to the court, that she had later formed the opinion that rather than it being asleep or unconscious, the baby might well have been dead.

The pair were finally brought to trial between the 15th and 16th January 1903 before Mr Justice Darling at the Old Bailey and after two days of evidence, the jury took around 40 minutes to declare them both guilty of the charges laid against them. It was reported that as the jury contained a number of women, a plea for leniency was made on behalf of the two women, but sadly for them it fell on deaf ears and Mr Justice Darling sentenced them both to death.

They were removed to Holloway Prison to await their fate on the morning of Tuesday 3rd February 1903. Later reports indicate that Walters was completely calm and at ease with herself throughout the remaining weeks of her life, unlike Sachs who was said to have been in a state of constant turmoil and telling anyone who would listen that she was entirely innocent.

On the day of their execution, William Billington assisted by Henry Pierrepoint entered the condemned cells at the appointed hour and quickly pinioned the prisoners arms. Walters was said to be fairly calm and compliant, whereas Sachs was reported to be in a state on near hysteria and had to be physically carried to the scaffold to join her fellow conspirator. Henry Pierrepoint later recalled;

"These two women were baby farmers of the worst kind and they were both equally repulsive in type. One was two pounds lighter than the other and there was a difference of two inches in the drop which I allowed. Sachs had a long thin neck and Walters a short neck, points I was bound to observe in the arrangement of the rope. They had to be literally carried to the scaffold and protested to the end against their sentences"

In more recent times it has been suggested that Sachs and Walters may have been the mysterious Browning women who were accused by the fated Louise Masset of murdering her young son Manfred. This is highly unlikely however, given that their methodology of murder is entirely different and the fact that Louise Masset was reported to have actually confessed to her crime as she waited in Newgate prison's condemned cell.

6. THE ABUSED WIFE

EMILY SWANN

Convicted of murdering her husband William Swann

This was yet another case where an extra-marital affair was to have fatal consequences, but in this instance, the death of the spouse appears to have the result of "hot blooded" rage, rather than any sort of cold blooded calculation.

Forty-two year old Emily Swann was said to be a mill worker in Wombwell, South Yorkshire, who along with her husband William was reported to have produced around eleven children as the result of a sometimes fraught and abusive marriage, which was perhaps typical of a time when male dominance, financial poverty and social deprivation were overriding factors in most working peoples lives.

Possibly to help alleviate their financial hardship, caused by low wages and a large number of mouths to feed, the Swann's were thought to have taken in a lodger called John Gallagher, who was a miner at one of the towns local collieries and looking to find accommodation close to his employment.

Although Emily was around twelve years older than him and had had a reported eleven children, the new lodger and his landlady soon began an illicit love affair, which almost inevitably soon became the subject of local gossip that finally came to the ears of Emily's husband, William. Determined to get to the truth of the rumours, the cheated husband was reported to have confronted the pair in a heated argument, which ultimately resulted in Gallagher leaving their home and moving out of the area.

Had that been the end of the matter, then no doubt all three parties would have gone on to live fairly anonymous lives and the affair would have soon been forgotten. However, it seems clear that John Gallagher continued to maintain contact with friends and neighbours in the town, perhaps checking on Emily's wellbeing and it was as the result of his visiting a former acquaintance in Wombwell that he and Emily were said to have had their fated meeting, which would result in a man being killed and the pair of lovers being condemned to death.

At the same time that Gallagher was making one of his infrequent visits to a mutual friend, it just happened that Emily called at the house carrying on her face the bruises that her husband had inflicted in his latest assault on his unfaithful wife. Outraged by the injuries, Gallagher was reported to have rushed out of the house, with Emily in hot pursuit, making his way into the Swann household, from where the neighbours could hear the banging and crashing of an obviously violent confrontation taking place between the two men.

After a few minutes the noise subsided and both Gallagher and Emily were reported to be out in the street, with the still incensed miner loudly threatening further physical harm to the wife beating husband who remained within the house. He was then said to have gone back inside the Swann's home with Emily, with the neighbours once again hearing the commotion of a violent struggle, but this time with the sound of Emily Swann urging her former lover to continue the attack and give her husband 'what for'.

Some few minutes after this second attack had started Gallagher and Emily once again left the house, only this time leaving her abusive husband lying dead in the wreckage, with a bloodied poker close by. The pair were then thought to have wandered back to the mutual friends house, arm-in-arm and calmly related the unseen events which had taken place inside the Swann's wrecked household.

Needless to say, the Police were called and having been made aware of the fracas and discovered the lifeless body of William Swann amidst the wreckage of his home, quickly arrested Emily Swann and charged her with being involved in the murder of her husband. Her accomplice, John Gallagher, had in the meantime made himself scarce however; and it was several weeks before the authorities were finally able to apprehend the vengeful paramour and charge him with the killing.

When they were final brought to trial at the Yorkshire Assizes in October of 1903, the pair were arraigned before Mr Justice Darling and jointly charged with the wilful murder of William Swann. The prosecution case clearly pointed to the fact that the ill-tempered and abusive husband had lost his life to a brutal and prolonged attack which was perpetrated by Gallagher, but with the complicity of Emily Swann, who tried to defend herself by claiming that she had not actively participated in the assault.

However, witnesses told the court of the two separate phases of the attack and of Emily's shouting encouragement to her lover as he battered her husband in the house. There was even a suggestion that she had actively taken part in the physical assault, but no direct evidence of this was put before the court. Gallagher freely admitted that he had gone to William Swann's house "to teach him a lesson", but denied that he ever had any intention of killing him, simply claiming that events had got out of control and the husband had inadvertently lost his life as a result of the violent struggle.

Unfortunately for him, witnesses claimed to have heard him threaten William's life both before the first part of the attack took place and then after he had come out into the street, before going back into the Swann's house for a second and final time. Clearly the jury came to the conclusion that the defendant had intended to kill the husband; and his subsequent actions proved that to be the case.

As for Emily Swann, the jury obviously concluded that she had played an equally active part in the murder, through her encouragement of the attack and the fact that she failed to stop Gallagher from continuing the attack on her husband even when he was no longer able to defend himself.

At the end of the trial and with all the evidence having been heard, the judge sent out the jury and they quickly came back with guilty verdicts on both defendants. The judge then had little option but to apply the mandatory death sentence to both prisoners, which were reported to have been received with little if any reaction by either Emily Swann or John Gallagher. It was later suggested that this lack of emotion was brought about by Emily's false belief that she would eventually have her sentence commuted and Gallagher's full expectation that he would hang for his actions anyway.

For Gallagher, there was to be no disappointment, but for Emily, the full horror of what awaited her only became plain once the full appeals process had been completed and the death sentence upheld. For the remaining weeks of her life, she was said to be a fairly tragic figure that had difficulty in maintaining her composure and getting her final affairs into some sort of order.

Finally, on the morning of the 29th December 1903, Emily was reported to be in a state of virtual collapse, verging on total hysteria and was said to have been supported by her prison guards, who were trying to persuade her to be strong. As William Billington the principal executioner entered the cell to pinion the distraught prisoner, it has been suggested that Emily was given a tot of brandy to help stiffen her resolve in her final moments. She was then led, supported by her guards, to the execution room where her lover John Gallagher was already standing, pinioned and hooded on the scaffold.

Considerably brightened by her shot of liquor, Emily was reported to have said "Good morning, John" as she was positioned on the gallows next to him. The somewhat surprised Gallagher, caught unawares by the suddenness of Emily's voice next to managed to mumble "Good morning, love".

Perhaps aware that there were only seconds to go, Emily was said to have called out "Goodbye, God bless you" before Billington pulled the lever that sent them both to their deaths, which were later reported to have been instantaneous.

7. THE LAST OF HER KIND

RHODA WILLIS

Convicted of murdering a young baby girl surnamed "Treasure"

There is perhaps nothing as catastrophic as a promising life that is given over to wasteful addiction; and that was particularly true for Rhoda Willis who went to her grave with the chilling epitaph of being the last baby farmer to hang in Britain.

Reported to have been born on the 14th August 1863, Willis was thought to have come from a relatively well-to-do family in the north-east of England, where she was given a decent education and later said to have married an upstanding and professional man, who was a marine engineer. Sadly for them both however, the marriage failed to last, although the precise reason for its failure is unclear.

Now separated from her husband and wider family, Willis was reported to have eventually drifted into South Wales, where it was said she was engaged as a housekeeper by a local Pontypool man called David Evans. Presumably to supplement her meagre income and perhaps to support her reputed drinking problem, she was said to have persuaded her employer to agree to her "adopting" babies, so that they could both earn a little more money; and so she began her first foray into the baby farming business. She was said to have placed an advertisement in the local Evening Press offering to adopt unwanted babies and gave a PO Box No. for interested parties to contact her.

On the 20th March 1907, a young unmarried mother called Emily Stroud was delivered of a generally healthy but unwanted baby and having seen the newspaper advert placed by Willis, arranged for both the child and the associated adoption fee to be handed over to the kindly woman. Unfortunately for everyone, Willis found herself incapable of looking after the new born infant and within a matter of days was devising a plan to rid herself of her new encumbrance. It was later proved that she had taken the baby to a local Salvation Army meeting house and abandoned it on the doorstep, leaving a note claiming that she was an unmarried mother who was unable to cope with the child and asking the Salvationists to take care of it. Sadly, either through her own incompetence or through just plain bad luck, the baby was not found in time and subsequently died from exposure, an event that would later come back to haunt the unfortunate Willis.

Whether she was aware of the first baby's death or not is unclear, but within a couple of weeks she was thought to have received further enquiries about her child adoption services which was still being advertised in the press. Around the 20th May 1907, Willis was reported to have adopted another baby that had recently been delivered, but fortunately the child's mother appears to have a change of heart or circumstance and retrieved the baby almost immediately. It may also have been around this time that she finally left the house of David Evans in Pontypool, perhaps because of her employer's growing unease or suspicions about her, or about the business that she had been running from his home.

Within a short time she was reported to be living in private lodgings in Cardiff, possibly supporting herself through her previous activities of petty theft and prostitution, both of which had inevitably brought her to the attention of the local authorities. Her growing alcoholism was said to be a notable factor in her choice of lifestyle and her landlady, Mrs Wilson, seems to have been used to her lodger staggering home drunk and having to be put to bed, because she was incapable through drunkenness.

Around the same time that Willis was inexorably drinking herself into oblivion, an acquaintance called Lydia English, who knew Willis under her alias of Leslie James and was aware of her baby adoption business, contacted her regarding her unmarried sister called Maud Treasure, who was pregnant and wanted to re-home her new, but illegitimate baby. English and Willis (James) discussed terms for the baby's adoption and eventually reached an agreement, whereby Willis would take the child for a fee of £6 and care for it. On the 4th June 1907 Willis was reported to have told her landlady that she was travelling to Bristol on "baby" business, a revelation that would later lead to the entirely innocent Mrs Wilson being accused of conspiracy in Willis' ultimately fatal baby farming activities.

The previous day Maude Treasure had finally delivered a baby girl, who she had agreed to place with Leslie James, the woman known to and recommended by her sister Lydia English. Willis duly arrived in Bristol on the 4th and having completed the financial side of the transaction, wrapped the one-day-old unnamed baby girl in a bundle and prepared to make her way back to her lodgings in Cardiff.

On the evening of the same day, Mrs Wilson saw and heard her lodger return from her trip to Bristol, much the worse for wear and carrying a bundle under her arm. A short time later she heard a heavy bump from Willis' room and went out to investigate, finding that her heavily intoxicated tenant had fallen out of bed and was lying on the floor of the bedroom. As she helped Willis back into bed, Mrs Wilson became aware of the bundle lying on the floor and having unwrapped it was horrified to discover the dead body of a newborn baby girl.

Immediately she contacted the Police and when the first officers arrived they quickly arrested the still inebriated Willis on suspicion of murdering the unknown baby girl. The child's body was subsequently removed to the local morgue, where a pathologist determined that the infant was no more than a day old and had died as a result of manual asphyxiation.

Once she had sobered up, Willis claimed that the baby had been in poor health and had died from natural causes, a defence which was easily undermined by the pathologist's own findings. The Police then began investigating Willis' past and soon discovered her previous history in the baby farming business, which inevitably linked them to the case of Emily Stroud's baby which had been abandoned outside the Salvation Army house and subsequently died from exposure. Taking a sample of Willis' handwriting, they asked an expert in the field to compare it against the note left with the dead baby, supposedly written by the unmarried mother that couldn't cope and the graphologist was later able to testify that both samples had in fact been written by the same hand.

Within three weeks of her arrest, Rhoda Willis was standing in the dock of Swansea Assizes charged with the murder of "Baby" Treasure, a case that would take just two days to complete. At the end of the second day, with the jury having heard the prosecution evidence against the accused woman and with Willis having no real defence against the charge, the jurors retired to consider their verdict. It only took them a short time to deliberate and within an hour they had returned to declare her guilty and it was then the trial judge's duty to impose the only possible sentence; death.

Willis' lawyers tried to appeal the sentence using the only defence that was open to them; that Willis was a chronic alcoholic and was drunk and incapable at the time that the baby died, so there could not have been any intent on her part to kill the child. Had it not been for the death of the Stroud baby, which had also died as a result of Willis' apparent negligence, perhaps the jury and the authorities might have accepted that the murder of "Baby" Treasure was entirely unintentional, but two children had died because of her actions and therefore no clemency was to be offered to the woman who had caused their deaths.

At eight o'clock on the morning of Wednesday 14th August 1907, Rhoda Willis' 44th birthday, Henry and Thomas Pierrepoint stepped into the condemned cell at Cardiff Prison and pinioned the arms of the petite and strikingly pretty woman they had been ordered to execute. Leading her across the open prison yard to the isolated execution shed, they placed her on the trapdoor of the scaffold, before completing the remaining procedures which would ultimately send the extremely sad, unhappy and unfortunate woman to an eternal peace.

It was reported that this particular execution and the prisoner herself had a profound effect on Henry Pierrepoint, perhaps because of her manner or simply because he realised what a pathetically unlucky individual she was to end up on the gallows. No-one, perhaps not even Willis herself, knew what happened on that final journey from Bristol to Cardiff that resulted in the one-day-old baby girl losing her life, but clearly alcohol addiction played a major part. Regardless of such reasons or excuses however, it was later stated that on the morning of her execution Rhoda Willis had freely admitted to causing and being responsible for the death of the child who forever would be known simply as "Treasure".

8. THE UNFAITHFUL INNOCENT

EDITH JESSIE THOMPSON

Convicted with Freddie Bywaters of murdering Percy Thompson

Born on the 25th December 1893, Edith Jessie Graydon was the first of five children born to William Graydon and his wife Ethel Jessie at the family's home at 97 Norfolk Road in Dalston, London. A bright and intelligent child Edith was said to be interested in music and dancing, as well as having an aptitude for arithmetic and a love of reading.

On leaving school she was reported to have gained a position as a book-keeper with a local fabrics importer and given her ability quickly rose through the office ranks to become a buyer for the company, a post which allowed her the opportunity to travel abroad and broaden her horizons.

Around 1909 she met her future husband, Percy Thompson, a rather reliable, conservative individual and after a fairly lengthy courtship the pair were finally married in 1916. Setting up home at Ilford in Essex, the successful and professional young couple were said to be able to live fairly comfortable lives, entertaining friends, going to the theatre and taking annual holidays.

Despite their fairly contented lives however, there is a sense that Edith found her existence staid and unexciting, caused in no small party by Percy, who by repute was said to be a rather conventional and predictable man, completely unlike his imaginative and highly receptive 27-year-old wife, who most would probably have considered to be an exception rather than the rule. Perhaps her regular trips to the continent had made her much more aware of the wider world and its infinite possibilities, than she found to be the case in the highly structured society of Victorian and Edwardian influenced Britain.

It was possibly this need for excitement and change that made her more susceptible to the charms of 20-year-old Freddie Bywaters, a merchant seaman that the couple became acquainted with in 1920. Edith was reported to have met him a few years earlier when Freddie attended the same school as one of her younger brothers, but now she saw him as a seafaring adventurer who interested her with his tales of foreign cultures and overseas adventures.

Percy Thompson too seemed to get on well with Freddie Bywaters and the couple were thought to have invited their new acquaintance to holiday with them and Edith's younger sister Avis on the Isle of Wight during the summer. The vacation was obviously a happy and successful one, as Percy was thought to have invited their new friend to lodge with them after the holiday, while he waited for his next ship to set sail. Although the arrangement was undoubtedly made with the best of intentions, unhappily for the three people involved it would inevitably have tragic consequences for them all.

Within a matter of weeks a deep attachment was said to have been formed between Edith and Freddy and although it was unclear whether or not the couple were actually sleeping together, for Percy Thompson the relationship was unacceptable and he was said to have ordered his new friend and lodger out of his home. For his part, Freddie was thought to have demanded that Percy release Edith from their marriage so that they might be together, which simply outraged the deceived husband even more. Although there is no suggestion that Percy was violent towards Edith on a regular basis, it was later reported that he was so angry and hurt about his wife's relationship with Bywaters, that he struck her several times and even physically threw her across the room, causing her some minor injuries.

Unfortunately for Percy Thompson, any hope that he had that his wife would soon forget Freddie Bywaters was a forlorn one, as Edith was thought to have simply maintained contact with her suitor behind her husbands back, either through letters or occasionally slipping away to a secret assignation. Even while Freddie was away at sea from September 1921 travelling the world, Edith was said to have stayed in constant communication, arranging for her love letters to be delivered to him onboard ship and telling him about her hopes, her fears and complaining about the dreariness of her daily life with Percy.

Obviously a gifted and evocative correspondent, Edith was thought to have used her love letters to Freddie as a way of fantasizing about how her seemingly humdrum life might be different if Percy wasn't in her life, even to the point of telling him that she had tried to kill her husband with ground up glass and poison, but then lamenting the fact that neither had worked. Bywaters simply regarded such claims as entirely fictional events, dreamt up by Edith both as an act of personal bravado and as an imaginary wish that she could never really commit.

Another aspect of these private letters, which would subsequently help to condemn Edith, was their unusually blunt references to her own feelings, both physical and emotional, especially when she recalled their lovemaking and how it made her feel. Generally unmentioned subjects such as her monthly periods, sexual orgasms were openly communicated, along with the routine of her everyday life, all of which she wanted to share with her lover who was so far away from her.

Returning to England in September 1922 Freddie was anxious to see Edith and the couple were thought to have arranged to meet one another at a secret location. Although there is no evidence to suggest that they actively colluded in subsequent events, perhaps Edith's continuing unhappiness was so evident and troubling to Freddie that he alone made the fateful decision to solve the problem once and for all.

The following month, on the evening of 3rd October 1922 Percy and Edith were returning home from a night out at the Criterion Theatre in Piccadilly Circus when they walked down a quiet side street in Ilford. Suddenly a figure leapt out from behind some bushes and knocked Edith to the ground, before turning to face Percy Thompson, after which a violent struggle ensued between the two men, while Edith struggled to regain her feet. As she became aware of the deadly battle she was heard to call out "No, don't" several times before rushing forward to catch hold of her fatally wounded husband, who fell to the floor bleeding profusely. As she attended to the dying Percy, the assailant fled the scene and within a matter of minutes local people and Police Officers began to arrive on the street to find out the cause of the commotion.

Discovering Percy's lifeless body lying in a pool of blood and Edith crying hysterically, the only thing that Officers could be sure of was that the couple, particularly the husband, had been the subjects of a violent and unprovoked attack, although the reason for the assault was as yet unclear. Detectives arranged for Percy's body to be taken to the local morgue and his grieving widow was brought to the local Police station to see if she could provide any clues, once she had been calmed down.

It has been suggested, that once at the station Edith had recovered sufficiently to answer questions put to her by the investigators and it was possibly as a result of this that she began to wonder if her lover Freddie Bywater had indeed played a part in the attack. Trying to be helpful, she suggested the possibility that her husband might have been attacked by a man she was involved with and was said to have fully detailed her illicit liaisons with Freddie, her husbands anger when he found out about their friendship and Freddie's determination that she should be free of her husband.

This explanation of events may indeed be true, although it has also been reported that it was the evidence of another lodger, Fanny Lester, who suggested that Freddie Bywaters was a likely suspect and told the Police about the relationship between Edith and her former lodger. Either way, the investigators now had a credible suspect in the shape of Freddie and within a short time had him in custody and had charged him with the murder of Percy Thompson.

It was while they were conducting a casual search of his rooms and belongings that detectives came across the bundle of 60-odd love letters that Edith Thompson had written to him, immediately raising the suspicion that she had somehow played a part in the crime. Further reading of this personal correspondence also brought to light Edith's imaginary attempts to kill her husband, her casual and apparently common recollections of socially unacceptable subject matter and the fact that she claimed to have aborted a child. Reported to have shocked even some of the hardened detectives who were involved with the case, the content of the letters would ultimately prove to be truly damning to a woman that was painted as being debased, vulgar and deliberately unconventional.

With the love letters as their only circumstantial evidence against her, the Police immediately arrested and charged Edith with being an accomplice in the capital murder of her husband Percy Thompson. Right from the start, the authorities were bound and determined to prove her guilty of "Common Consent", suggesting that although she had not struck the fatal blow; she had played an equal part in suggesting or planning the murder, making her equally guilty in the eyes of the law. To that end and following the discovery of her letters, which stated that she had fed Percy ground glass as well as poison, the authorities ordered the dead mans body exhumed so that a full autopsy could be carried out. Unfortunately for the prosecutors, despite the attentions of two of the country's top pathologists, there was no evidence to substantiate Edith's claims, proving to most observers that she was indeed making the whole thing up.

As soon as he had been arrested and charged with Percy Thompson's murder, Freddie had proved to be an extremely truthful and helpful suspect, even leading Officers to the exact spot where he had disposed of the bloodied murder weapon. But when questioned about Edith and any part she had played in the crime he was resolute, she had known nothing, had played no part and it was as simple and as straightforward as that.

Regardless of his protestations however, both Freddie and Edith were brought to trial for the murder of her husband Percy at the Old Bailey on 6th December 1922. Although the prosecution had little in the way of direct evidence against Edith and despite the advice of her defence counsel for her not to testify in open court, she disregarded the expert's advice and ended up helping to condemn herself.

Caught out in a series of damning lies and deliberately refusing to answer questions that were put to her by the prosecuting counsel, Edith somehow managed to present herself to the court as being a dishonest, evasive and highly melodramatic individual who did not endear herself to the jury. She was even reported to have contradicted several witnesses, whose evidence in normal circumstances would have helped her case, but because of her own erratic performance in the witness box, much of this testimony was overlooked or ignored by the jurors who would later convict her.

Unlike Edith, Freddie Bywaters was thought to have presented himself as a highly competent witness who tried to defend his actions by claiming that he never intended to kill Percy Thompson, but merely to reason with him and demand that he release Edith from their obviously ruined marriage. However, on the night in question, having confronted the husband, he was so angered by Percy's condescending attitude and provocative behaviour that the two men inevitably came to blows and it was as a result of this totally unexpected fight that Percy had died. In the witness box he totally refuted any suggestion that he and Edith had conspired together to murder her husband or that she had deliberately guided Percy to that particular street, in order for him to be waylaid by Freddie.

When questioned about the love letters and their references to the attempts on Percy's life, as well as Edith's request that he do "something to help her", Freddie simply dismissed the entries as fantasies written by his highly imaginative and extremely unhappy lover. He categorically denied that Edith had any prior knowledge of the evening's events, which he committed alone, but without any intention of killing Percy Thompson.

Despite his honest recollections and his stalwart defence of Edith, the love letters which had been written to him remained a crucially important part of the Crown's case against them both. Because of the content, some of which was deemed to be unsuitable for reading by the jurors, many of the letters were reported to have been censored in such a way, as to completely alter their context and meaning. Consequently, they could easily be misinterpreted by those that read them, including the judge who called them "vulgar" and members of the jury, one of whom was recorded to have described them as "nauseas".

The trial judge, Mr Justice Shearman, when summing up the case for the jury, prior to their being sent out to consider a verdict, managed to remind the jurors that they had to be wholly convinced of Edith Thompson's involvement in or knowledge of the crime, in order to convict her of the charge which she now faced. However, it was also reported that Justice Shearman's obvious dislike and disgust of the prisoners illicit relationship and in particular Edith's unconventional, almost pornographic writings, was clearly conveyed to all that were sitting in the court as well as the jury who were due to consider their guilt or innocence.

It perhaps only came as a surprise to Edith Thompson and Freddie Bywaters when the jury returned some two hours later, on the 11th December 1922, with guilty verdicts on both prisoners. On hearing the verdict Edith was reported to have become hysterical and Freddie began shouting that she was entirely innocent of the crime. Regardless of his own feelings about the verdicts, Justice Shearman was reported to have thanked the jury, before imposing the maximum sentence on the man and woman who stood in the dock before him. With the death penalty imposed, the two prisoners were then taken down, ready for transportation to their respective prisons where they would spend the final few weeks of their lives and where the executions would take place.

As she waited for her transport to Holloway Prison, Edith was held in a cell below the court and was allowed to see members of her family there. As her father came into the room she was said to have rushed into his arms and pleaded with him to take her home, something he was plainly unable to do.

With Edith incarcerated at Holloway and Freddie at nearby Pentonville Prison, there was reported to have been a complete turnaround in public opinion and interest in the two ill-fated lovers. During the trial it seems that many people believed the pair guilty of murder, but following Freddie's convincing and continuing defence of Edith, more and more people came to accept that she probably was innocent of murder, but entirely guilty of adultery and having an illegal abortion, but did not deserve to be hung for those unconventional acts. Many British people were also thought to have come to the conclusion that although Freddie Bywaters had admitted killing Percy Thompson, perhaps events had transpired the way he had stated in court and he hadn't intended to murder the victim. Possibly with these considerations in mind, nearly one million people were said to have signed a petition calling for the pair to be reprieved, but the government of the day and the Home Secretary William Bridgeman resisted all calls for clemency and ordered that the executions should go ahead regardless.

Although Freddie was said to have had little expectation that he would be reprieved, Edith did think her sentence would be commuted, probably because she was entirely innocent of the crime. So when the Governor of Holloway informed her that there would be no reprieve and that her execution was to go ahead, she was reported to have lost her mind completely and spent the remaining days of her life in a constantly hysterical state, refusing to eat and crying continuously.

On the morning of the 9th January 1923, at both Holloway and Pentonville Prison's, two of Britain's official executioners and their assistants stepped into the condemned cells to carry out the sentences imposed by the courts. At Pentonville, William Willis had the much easier task of pinioning Freddie Bywaters who was reported to have been compliant and extremely brave as he was prepared for the gallows. John Ellis on the other hand, had entered the condemned cell at Holloway to find his female prisoner in a state of total physical collapse and having to be supported by her warders. With the added assistance of his two deputies, Robert Baxter and Seth Mills, Ellis was able to pinion the weeping woman, who then had to be carried to and supported on the scaffold as he placed the white hood over her head and the noose about her neck. Moving quickly, Ellis released the retaining pin and pulled the lever which brought an instantaneous end to Edith Thompson's earthly suffering, but at the same time beginning a judicial mystery which remains with us to this day. Half a mile away and around the same time Freddie Bywaters was known to have suffered a similar fate, perhaps aware in those final seconds that it was his own impulsive thoughts and actions which had conspired to bring him and Edith only death and disaster, instead of the happiness they had both wanted so badly.

For the unfortunate hangmen who had been asked to carry out the highly distressing execution there was reported to be one final shocking incident which caused them all to remember Edith Thompson's death for the rest of their lives. Charged with preparing her body for the mandatory autopsy, as they took her lifeless corpse down from the gallows they noticed that the prisoner had suffered some sort of major haemorrhage which had left blood all over her lower extremities and her underwear. Official sources later claimed that no such "untoward" event took place, but it seems likely that there was a bleed of some description that deeply shocked the normally composed executioner, Ellis, who was known to have officially retired from his post the following year. Despite the authority's denials, it seems a huge coincidence that following Edith's execution all condemned female prisoners were required to wear canvas knickers in order that there was no reoccurrence of such a phantom event.

Following her execution and autopsy Edith's body was interred within the precincts of Holloway Prison, where it would lie undisturbed for nearly 50 years, alongside the likes of Amelia Sachs and Annie Walters. In 1971, as the prison was undergoing a major rebuilding programme, Edith's remains, along with those of Sachs, Walters and Styllou Christofi were reinterred at the massive Brookwood Cemetery in Surrey, where in later years a proper gravestone was added to help identify the fated women that are buried there.

Even after the executions of Edith Thompson and Freddie Bywaters, the public furore over the case refused to subside, caused in no small part by a growing belief that an entirely innocent woman had been hanged largely for her morals, rather than for any criminal act that she had committed. Rather than make their case to the public, the government of the day simply reinforced the idea of a cover-up by ordering the case papers to be sealed for 100 years, preventing any sort of independent study or investigation which might settle Edith Thompson's guilt or innocence once and for all.

9. A QUICK TEMPERED WOMAN

SUSAN NEWELL

Convicted of murdering 13 year-old newspaper boy John Johnson

Reported to have been born sometime between 1893 and 1895, Susan McAllister was one of 13 children belonging to Peter McAllister, an itinerant tinsmith and his wife Janet, both of whom were thought to have spent their entire lives travelling, settling only occasionally to earn a living or to add to their ever growing brood.

Sometime before the outbreak of war Susan was said to have married a man called Robert McLeod, to whom she delivered a baby daughter, Janet, in 1915. Seven years later, her first husband was dead and Susan McLeod was reported to have married John Newell, who by reputation was a womanising drunk and a less than adequate provider for his short-tempered wife and her young eight-year-old daughter.

By the end of May 1923 the Newell family were thought to have recently moved into new lodgings at 2 Newlands Street, Coatbridge, the building being owned by a widow called Mrs Annie Young. It is entirely likely that the Newell's had moved there, having been given notice to quit by their previous landlord and given the reported volatility of the relationship between Susan and John Newell this was probably a regular occurrence.

Within three weeks of having moved into their new home their stormy and noisy relationship had already brought their landlady to the limits of her patience and almost inevitably around the middle of June 1923 she told the family that they would have to leave. This announcement just simply sparked even more resentment and recriminations between the warring couple and eventually John was said to have had enough and basically abandoned his wife and her daughter while he went off to find some peace and quiet. It would later transpire however, that even then the highly irascible wife was not content to sit at home and wait for him to return, but instead tracked him down and demanded that he return home immediately. When he refused to come back, the combative wife was reported to head-butted him before storming off back to their lodgings at Coatbridge.

The 20th June 1923 found Susan Newell and her daughter Janet still inside their lodgings, penniless and still facing the prospect of having to find new accommodation for themselves. Undoubtedly, her tenuous situation and the violent argument with her erstwhile and still absent husband had pushed her to the brink of reason, but even that was a poor excuse for the events which were to follow.

Thirteen-year-old John Johnson was said to helping a friend sell newspapers when he made the fatal mistake of knocking on Susan Newell's front door at around 6.50 pm that evening. Although the full details of the killing were only ever known to the victim and his murderer, it was later speculated that the young paper boy had objected to Newell taking one of his papers without paying for it and that either through a remark or threat made by John, the extremely irate woman had first beat the boy to the floor before strangling him to death.

With the murdered boy's body lying on her apartment floor, Newell did not seem to panic about her situation, but calmly set about picking up the lifeless John Johnson before laying his corpse on the family's couch. When her young daughter Janet returned from playing with friends, her mother simply called on her landlady Mrs Annie Young and asked if she had a box that she could use to pack up some of her belongings, in readiness for the family leaving the property. Although Mrs Young had seen the newspaper boy call at her lodger's door, she just assumed that he had subsequently left the building and no mention was made of him by Mrs Newell.

Having had a brief conversation with her landlady Susan Newell was then said to have returned to her rooms, before going out with her daughter to a local bar to fetch a jug of beer. Janet McLeod would testify at her mother's trial that they had gone out to the local bar, where she had to wait outside, while her mother went inside to buy a jug of beer. Having got her drink, the couple then returned to their rooms where Susan was reported to have sat down and got drunk, staring at the lifeless body of the newspaper boy, before finally covering his face with a pair of her husband's drawers.

By the following morning and with the crime still undiscovered, the murderous housewife had finally devised a method to remove the boy's body from her rooms and she quickly set her plan in motion. With the help of young Janet she was said to have wrapped John's body in a bed quilt and placed it in an old pram that had been left standing in the hallway and finally having sat her daughter atop the deadly bundle, she set off to dispose of the problem. Fortunately for her, she had just left her rooms to begin her journey when landlady Mrs Young came out of her apartment to fetch her morning milk, noticing only that the Newell's front door had been left ajar, before she went back in to begin her daily chores.

As Newell hurriedly pushed the heavy load along the main road in Coatbridge, a local lorry driver called Thomas Gibson noticed the woman and her daughter and stopped to offer them a lift into the city. The woman asked to be dropped at Duke Street in Glasgow and having arrived there he tried to help her off-load the pram containing the bundle, but she curtly refused his offer and manhandled it onto the pavement alone.

What the lorry driver had failed to notice, was that the bundle in the pram had loosened as a result of it being jostled and John Johnson's head and one of his feet had been exposed, although were quickly covered over again by the seeming unflustered Newell. Unfortunately for her, a local woman Helen Elliot was far more observant than Gibson and had seen the extremities of the boy exposed and quickly located a local policeman to tell about the woman with a body in her pram.

Perhaps to get off the main thoroughfare, Susan Newell had chosen a small close to dispose of the body and as she made her way back, found herself confronted by the policeman who had first been alerted by Helen Elliot. Taking hold of the nervous woman, the officer began a search of the general area and quickly discovered the body of young John Johnson and immediately arrested the woman on suspicion of his murder. Taken to Tobago Street Police Station, Susan Newell then set about trying to implement her backup plan, which was deliberately designed to implicate her entirely innocent husband John in the murder, leaving her as the dutiful wife and mother who had accidentally become involved in the disposal of the body, but was entirely innocent of any part in the crime itself.

She calmly told the investigating officers of the previous night's events, of how the young newspaper boy had called at the apartment while she and her husband were arguing and how John Johnson had cried out when her husband had struck her. She then recalled her horror as her husband took hold of the boy and throttled him until "his face was black", leaving his lifeless body on the floor of their lodgings. Purely to save her spouse's life she had decided to dispose of the body, somewhere away from their rooms, so that no suspicion could be attached to her family.

When the Police questioned the only other potential witness to the crime, Newell's eight-year-old daughter Janet, she corroborated her mother's story, of how John Newell had killed the boy and she and her mother were simply moving the body so that they wouldn't be blamed. Susan Newell had evidently coached her daughter well enough to fool the Police in the short term, with them quickly issuing an arrest warrant for the missing John Newell, but ultimately the young girl's fabricated tale soon began to unravel and before long she was telling Detectives the true story of the night before.

In the meantime, the Police had contacted John Johnson's father, who had reported his son missing the night before. Leaving work early, the emotionally shattered Robert Johnson was asked to attend Glasgow Central's Police Mortuary where he had to perform the grim task of formally identifying the body of his 13-year-old son John, before going home to tell his distraught wife that their beloved son was dead.

The grieving father would later tell officers of the previous day's events, of how his boy had gone out to help a pal sell some newspapers and that when he failed to return home, he and his wife had simply assumed the John and his friends had gone to the pictures. However by 10.30 pm, when the pictures had closed and his son had still not come home Robert had become increasingly worried about his son. He had reported the matter to the Police and then spent the rest of the evening and early hours of the next morning wandering the streets trying to find his son, stopping only to return home, to see if the boy had turned up in the meantime.

Within days of the discovery of the boy's dead body and with the story having been carried by all of the local and national newspapers, the missing husband, John Newell, presented himself at a local Police station and was promptly taken in for questioning. The undoubtedly shocked man was able to tell detectives that he had in fact left the family home some days before the murder and had not returned there since. He related how a few days before the crime, he and his wife had been given notice to quit their accommodation by their landlady, how he and Susan Newell had had a blazing row and how he had subsequently abandoned her and Janet simply to visit relatives and get some peace and quiet.

A couple of days after leaving Susan, he was visiting friends in Parkhead when his wife managed to track him down, demanding that he return at once to Coatbridge to support her and Janet. However, when he refused to go back with her, his wife had head-butted him in the face before storming off and presumably returning to the family home. On the 20th June, the day of the murder, he told the interviewing officers, he had been at a bar in the East End of Glasgow before visiting his sister and then the following day he had travelled to the East Lothian area where he intended to stay for a while. It was only after he had read about the boy's death and the fact that he was a wanted man that he decided to return home to help the Police with their enquiries.

Detectives were pretty quickly able to substantiate John Newell's record of his movements before, during and after the murder, so inevitably began to focus their full attention on the only other logical suspect that could have committed the crime, Susan Newell. By carefully questioning eight-year-old Janet, the only other potential witness to the night's events, Detectives soon began to reveal the true sequence of events that had taken place in the Newell's apartment and exposing the supposedly innocent wife as the true killer.

Both John and Susan Newell were arraigned for trial at the Central Court House, Glasgow on the 18th September 1923, but almost immediately evidence was put before the court proving John's innocence and the Judge ordered him discharged, at the same time publicly criticising the prosecution services for having put the entirely guiltless man in the dock in the first place. As he stepped down to his freedom, it was noted by many in the court that the falsely accused man deliberately avoided looking at his estranged wife who now sat in the dock facing the charge alone.

Perhaps perversely, the main prosecution witness who would testify against Susan Newell was the very person who she had hoped would help her escape any sort of suspicion, her own daughter Janet. Her truthful recollections of the nights events, allied to the testimony of the many other witnesses who were called, painted the picture of a woman who seemed to have lost all reason, both through natural temperament and possibly through intoxication, which allowed her to kill an entirely innocent young boy for the cost of a daily newspaper.

With no alternative motive or reason to put forward, Newell's defence counsel T. A. Gentles KC tried to plead that his client had committed the act while she was insane, pointing out that there was no evidence of premeditation or indeed motive. However, the prosecution's own psychiatric expert told the court that he had examined Newell while she was held on remand and had found no evidence of mental incapacity and in his opinion she was perfectly sane.

At the end of a trial which had gripped and horrified the public imagination, the jury were sent out by the judge to consider their verdict, only to return some 37 minutes later with a unanimous decision of guilty. However, there was also a unanimous plea for clemency from the juror's, suggesting that most, if not all of them, believed that there were extenuating circumstances which needed to be taken into account and that perhaps Susan Newell was indeed suffering from some sort of mental illness.

Regardless of the jury's plea however, the judge was not so easily convinced or inclined to spare a woman who had taken the life of an entirely innocent youngster and perhaps shocked many in the court be imposing the maximum sentence, the death penalty. As for Susan Newell herself, later reports seemed to suggest that on receiving the sentence she was indifferent to it and simply turned on her heels and calmly walked down the steps of the dock to the waiting cells below.

In the subsequent days and weeks following the outcome of the trial there was an extensive and fairly high profile campaign to have Susan Newell's death sentence commuted. Unfortunately for Newell and her supporters her case became embroiled in a political debate, focusing on the implementation of the law in both England and Scotland and in which the Secretary of State for Scotland found himself inextricably involved. Less than a year before Newell's case, Edith Thompson had been executed in England for her part in the murder of her husband, although grave doubts still exist to this day, as to her actual guilt. Nonetheless, the fact that the English Home Secretary had refused to spare Thompson from the gallows, inevitably put pressure on his Scottish counterpart to adopt a similar hard-line approach to those people found guilty of a capital crime in Scotland. Possibly as a direct consequence of these political considerations, eventually the Scottish Secretary decided that Susan Newell should die for the murder of 13-year-old John Johnson, becoming the first woman executed in Scotland for 50 years.

On the morning of the 10th October 1923, John Ellis and his assistant Robert Baxter entered Newell's condemned cell at Duke Street Prison in Glasgow and set about pinioning the doomed woman's arms to her sides. Whether through haste or lack of concentration, Ellis had not tightened the wrist straps properly and having led her to the gallows, placed the rope around her neck, he then covered her head with the traditional white hood. Suddenly, Newell struggled free from her wrist restraints and pulled the hood from her head, telling the undoubtedly startled executioner "Don't put that thing on me". The unexpected interruption does not appear to have prevented Ellis from completing his task however and he quickly removed the retaining pin, pulled the lever and sent a bare-faced Susan Newell into the waiting void below and to an almost instantaneous death.

Although she was never reported to have admitted her guilt for the murder of John Johnson, Susan Newell was almost certainly the person responsible for the killing of the 13-year-old newspaper boy. That having been said, it seems equally clear that she committed the crime while she was in a rage, rather than in a deliberate or cold-blooded state of mind and as her counsel argued there was little evidence to suggest premeditation or indeed motive in her actions. In other circumstances and with a different political climate Susan Newell may well have had her death sentence commuted to a custodial sentence, however given her highly irascible and violent nature it seems extremely unlikely that she would have gone on to live a peacefully anonymous life.

10. FOOTWEAR TO DIE FOR

LOUIE CALVERT

Convicted of murdering her employer Mrs Lily Waterhouse

Reported to have been born in 1893, Louie Calvert was thought to be a true product of the tough Yorkshire working classes that she was born into, with limited means, little education and even less prospects of escaping the violence and poverty which were common factors in her own society.

Not blessed with handsome good looks or indeed a lovable nature, Louie was said to have made her way through life by working in a series of manual, low-paid jobs, committing the occasional petty theft and occasionally selling herself on the streets of her home city. Needless to say, it was probably as a result of these less than legitimate activities that she inevitably came to the attention of the Police and began to adopt a number of different identities, including that of Louise Jackson and Louie Gomersal.

It was as Louise Jackson, that around 1925 she took on the post of housekeeper to a night watchman called Arthur Calvert and it wasn't long before their relationship was said to have become much more intimate. Within a few months of the relationship having started Louie was thought to have announced to her new partner that she was pregnant with his child and suggesting that they should marry. Clearly, Arthur Calvert was prepared to "do the right thing" and soon after he and Louie were known have settled down as man and wife.

As the weeks and months passed however, the matter of the new baby and its impending birth was thought to have become an issue between the couple, perhaps because of Louie's failure to show any signs of being pregnant or her avoidance of the subject generally. Whatever the precise reasons, at the beginning of March 1926 Louie was thought to have told her possibly suspicious husband that she was going to stay with a sister in Dewsbury to have the new baby, no doubt explaining that her sister could help with the delivery of the child and any other medical care she required.

In fact Louie simply travelled to Leeds and quickly found lodgings in a private boarding house, run by an eccentric 40-year-old widow called Mrs Lily Waterhouse, who just happened to be in need of a live-in housekeeper-cum-maid and so the newly arrived Mrs Calvert was only too happy to take on the role. Shortly afterwards, Louie was thought to have seen a newspaper advert for a child that needed adopting and perhaps recognising that this might solve her problem in respect of Arthur Calvert, she made arrangements to adopt the baby from its mother and then brought it back to Mrs Waterhouse' boarding house.

Unfortunately for Louie, it appears that she wasn't a very good housekeeper in the first place and the fact that she now had an infant to look after meant that she did even less work around the house, which was thought to have become a real bone of contention between the two women. Possibly realising that there was no long-term future with the oddly behaving Lily Waterhouse, Louie was said to have begun stealing items from her employer and pawning the stolen goods to raise money, ready for her almost inevitable departure. Sadly for her, the widow began to suspect that things were going missing and having searched through Louie's belongings found several pawnbrokers redemption slips, which proved that her housekeeper was indeed taking items from the house and selling them for cash.

No doubt hurt and angry by the thefts perpetrated by her ungrateful employee and rather than confronting Louie directly, Lily Waterhouse was thought to have reported the matter to the local Police who told her that they would pass the complaint on to detectives who would no doubt contact her in due course to investigate the matter more fully.

Having travelled back from the Police Station, Mrs Waterhouse was later noticed by neighbours as she arrived back at her boarding house and once again the following morning, but after that, the eccentric landlady was never seen again. On the evening of the same day, her neighbours suddenly became aware of a series of loud thuds and the sound of what appeared to be Mrs Waterhouse moaning, but no-one was sufficiently alarmed to go and investigate the unusual noises. Sometime later Louie Calvert was seen to leave the Waterhouse property carrying her baby and as she left one of the neighbours was thought to have called out to inquire about the strange sounds. The housekeeper simply replied that the baby's cot had collapsed as she tried to dismantle it and the moaning was caused by Mrs Waterhouse being upset by the news that Louie and the baby were leaving her home.

Seemingly satisfied by the woman's explanation the neighbour simply bade the housekeeper farewell and went back to pursuing their earlier chore or routine and presumably thinking little more about the matter. The next day however, the same neighbours would have been equally intrigued to see two men peering through the windows of the boarding house and appearing to receive no answer to their knocking on the door, or calling the landlady's name.

The strangers, subsequently identified as Police detectives had called to interview Mrs Waterhouse about her complaint regarding the theft of her belongings by the housekeeper and were concerned to find the property completely locked up and seemingly uninhabited. Fortunately, a neighbour was able to furnish them with a spare front door key and the two officers were finally able to gain access to the house which they entered with some trepidation.

A cursory search of the property soon revealed the lifeless body of Mrs Waterhouse, lying in one of the smaller upstairs bedrooms, the corpse displaying the evidence of her having been beaten around the head, as well as ligature marks on her neck and wrists. For one of the detectives, the fact that the dead woman had been found bare-footed was also noteworthy, as it reminded him of another case in which he had been involved some four years earlier.

Having spoken to the neighbours, it soon became evident that the last person to see Mrs Waterhouse alive was the accused housekeeper and it therefore seemed logical to officers that she must be the prime suspect in the vicious murder of her employer. Within a relatively short time the detectives had tracked Louie down to her home at Railway Place in Leeds, where she had returned to her husband Arthur Calvert along with their new baby. When they knocked on the door, it was the wanted woman herself who answered, wearing a pair of boots which were quite evidently several sizes too big for her and which would later be proved to have belonged to the dead landlady.

Explaining that they were investigating the murder of Mrs Waterhouse, the officers undertook a brief search of the Calvert's home and quickly found several items of property that they believed had been stolen from her former employer. Louie tried to defend herself by telling the detectives, that Lily had in fact given her the items to pawn on her behalf, but because of the landlady's usual forgetfulness she had undoubtedly become confused over the matter. The Policemen were not to be fooled however and regardless of any theft charges that might have arisen from these items being recovered, they were fairly sure that they had the killer of Lily Waterhouse in their custody and immediately arrested Louie on suspicion of murdering the dead woman.

Initially remanded at Armley Prison in the city, Louie was finally brought to trial at Leeds Assizes on the 5th and 6th May 1926, where after a two day court case she was found guilty of murdering the 40-year-old Lily Waterhouse. With the prisoner condemned by the jury, the judge Mr Justice Wright had few reservations about imposing the mandatory death sentence on the woman that stood in the dock before him, who was said to have been received notice of the death penalty with an air of calm indifference.

Clearly though, she had given the possibility of being executed some thought and shortly after being condemned to death she was said to have told the authorities that she was in the early stages of pregnancy, raising the likelihood that an entirely innocent child might well be killed in the process of executing its mother. Although a physical examination of Louie Calvert proved to be inconclusive, on balance the authorities took the view that the claims were a complete fabrication by the condemned woman and ordered that the sentence should be carried out regardless.

The Parliamentary record, Hansard 22nd June 1926, notes that two days before her execution a Dr Watts asked whether the prisoner Louie Calvert, who was currently under sentence of death was in a state of pregnancy. In reply to the question, Sir William Joynson Hicks the Secretary of State replied that any doubts about her condition had been dispelled and it was certain there was no pregnancy.

Perhaps realising that she could not escape the gallows, Louie was reported to have finally admitted her guilt for the murder of Mrs Waterhouse to detectives and perhaps surprised the investigators by also confessing to the murder, four years earlier, of her former employer John Frobisher whose body had been found in a local canal cutting. Although she had been a potential suspect in that particular crime, detectives had been unable to find any conclusive evidence against her and so the case had remained unsolved and might have remained so, had Louie not decided to clear her conscience once and for all.

For one particular detective, Louie's death cell confession finally resolved the one obvious similarity between the two apparently unrelated murders, that of the victims missing footwear. When John Frobisher's body had been dragged from the water in 1922, the officers were struck by the fact that the victim was not wearing any shoes or boots and despite their best efforts to locate the footwear close to the scene, none were ever found. Although Frobisher's death was ultimately deemed to be accidental, the fact that his boots were missing remained a perplexing oddity of the case.

So when the same detective noticed that Lily Waterhouse' lifeless body was missing its footwear, it may well have sparked a memory of the earlier case within the investigators mind and helped him to make a connection between the two supposedly unconnected events. As it turned out, the link between the two bodies appears to have been Louie Calvert's obsession with the victim's footwear, which she obviously considered to be intrinsically valuable and much too important to leave with the corpses.

At nine o'clock in the morning, an hour later than was usual, on the 24th June 1926 Thomas Pierrepoint and his assistant William Willis stepped into the condemned cell at Manchester Strangeway's Prison and began the execution process that within a matter of minutes would send Louie Calvert to a painless and almost instantaneous death. Her body, having hung for the mandatory hour was late taken down and an autopsy performed which proved unequivocally that the condemned woman had indeed lied about her condition and was not in fact carrying a child when she died. Her remains were eventually interred in a plot within the prison precincts.

11. THE SCORNED AND LETHAL WIFE

ETHEL MAJOR

Convicted of murdering her husband Arthur Major

When Ethel Lillie Brown married local soldier, Arthur Major, who had been wounded during one of the many battles of the First World War, neither one of them could possibly have imagined that their subsequent 16 year relationship would eventually end with mutual suspicion, hatred and death. How different their lives might have been, had Ethel not decided to keep a deep and dark secret from her new husband, which would ultimately lead them both to disaster.

Reported to have been born sometime around 1891, Ethel was thought to have been a fairly plain country girl who made the mistake of getting herself pregnant through having an illicit affair with an obviously unavailable man, but later found herself unexpectedly rescued by her own parents. Rather than putting the baby girl who was called Auriel, up for adoption, Ethel's parents took the child as their own and as far as the world was concerned, Ethel and Auriel were sisters, not mother and daughter. So when Ethel and Arthur Major met and married in around 1918, as far as the groom was concerned, their own baby boy Lawrence, who was born within 12 months of their marriage, was the first and only child that either husband or wife had had.

However, some 14 or 15 years later rumours began to circulate around their home village that maybe the relationship between Ethel and her sister Auriel wasn't quite what it purported to be and before long this gossiping had reached the ears of Arthur Major, who was reported to be working in a local quarry. The outraged husband quickly confronted his wife about the allegations and although she initially denied the rumours, eventually admitted to him that Auriel was indeed her daughter, but refused outright to name the father, which as far as Arthur was concerned was a deceit too far.

Their marriage and relationship immediately began to disintegrate and it wasn't long before their home life became a routine round of bickering, threats and maliciously gossiping about one another around their local village and amongst their mutual friends. Things were said to be so bad, that often Ethel would walk several miles with her son Lawrence to go and stay at her parents home, rather than spend an evening listening to her husband's continuing taunts and accusations.

The situation changed markedly though, when the village rumour mill began to suggest that Arthur was having a relationship with a local woman, Rose Kettleborough, who was said to be a neighbour of the couple, a rumour which was later thought to have been substantiated by Ethel when she found two letters from the woman in her husband's possession. Incandescent with rage, Ethel was reported to have told her family doctor "A man like him isn't fit to live and I'll do him in".

Around the beginning of 1934, the previously fit and well Arthur Major was reported to have begun suffering from bouts of illness, including having fits, which although mysterious, did not seem to overly concern his local GP. However, in the May of that year his illness seemed to have got progressively worse and at 10:30 pm on the evening of the 24th May 1934 he was said to have died at home, presumably as a result of his recurring illness.

It seems clear that there was little if any suspicion about the cause of Arthur Major's death and had it not been for an anonymous letter sent to the authorities then he would have been simply buried and soon forgotten about. Within days of his death being reported however, the local authorities were told about the sudden and unexplained death of a neighbours dog who it was rumoured had died around the same time, possibly as the result of being fed by someone in the Major's household.

The coincidence was not lost on the recipient and the local Horncastle Police under the leadership of Detective Inspector Hodson were immediately informed and began to investigate the matter. The body of the neighbour's dog was exhumed and it was reported that Arthur Majors funeral was halted by the Police, in order that further investigations could be carried out. Tissue samples from both were analysed by the noted Home Office pathologist Dr Roche Lynch, who very quickly found evidence of Strychnine in both sets of samples and immediately advised the Horncastle Police that Arthur Major had in fact been murdered.

With the possibility of a Capital Offence having been committed, leadership of the case was said to have been handed over to Chief Inspector Young of Lincolnshire Police who immediately began to investigate the most obvious suspect, Ethel Lillie Major, the murdered man's wife. He soon became aware of the highly fraught and irreconcilable nature of the Major's marriage, the truth about Auriel's true parentage and Arthur Major's suspected affair with his neighbour. Further enquiries also brought to light Ethel's prior knowledge of her husbands affair and her reported remarks to her doctor, as well as the fact that she had access to Strychnine through her elderly father, Thomas Brown, who was a former gamekeeper and kept the poison as a method of controlling vermin.

Although the Strychnine at her father's home was reported to have been kept safely locked away, it has been suggested that a key to the box containing the poison was later found in Ethel Major's purse, proving conclusively that she did indeed have full access to the lethal materials.

It would later transpire that both Arthur Major and the unfortunate dog had eaten the same Corned Beef which had been previously laced with the deadly poison, with the unsuspecting husband giving the "badly tasting" meat to the neighbour's dog presumably as an act of kindness, rather than with any sort of wicked intent. This same meat was later proved by Police to have been purchased by the Major's 15-year-old son Lawrence at his mother's expressed instruction.

The most damning evidence however, was thought to have come from Ethel Major herself when she was formally interviewed by Chief Inspector Young regarding her husband's death. She was reported to have stated "I've never had any Strychnine poison" before being reminded by the officer that he had never once mentioned Strychnine in their interview. Ethel then tried to retrieve the situation by saying "Sorry, I must have made a mistake". Indeed she had, the Police later arresting and charging her with the murder of her husband.

Brought to trial at Lincoln Assizes in October 1934, Ethel Major's case was said to have lasted four days before the jury retired for an hour, before bringing back a verdict of guilty of murder. Perhaps considerate of the emotional maelstrom that she had lived in for the previous months and the bitter and irascible nature of her dead husband, the jury were also reported to have attached a plea for clemency to the judge, which he himself would later support in his case report to the Home Secretary. However, given the verdict on the day, the judge had little option but to implement the required penalty against the prisoner and issued the death penalty to the woman that stood condemned before him.

Having been taken down Ethel was immediately returned to Lincoln Prison, before being moved to the condemned cell at Hull Prison where her execution was due to take place on the 19th December 1934. Despite the concurrence of the judge with the jury's plea for mercy, the Home Secretary of the time was not inclined to reprieve Ethel Major and despite this recommendation and other campaigns to have the Lincolnshire housewife spared, ultimately the death sentence was upheld.

This and other poisoning cases seems to support the view that Britain's political establishment have always taken the position that murderers who use poisons as a weapon of choice, typically women, did not have their death sentences commuted. This possibly reflects the idea, that because poisoning is often a deliberate, lengthy and sometimes tortuous method of killing their victim, that the person perpetrating the act is far less worthy of pity or forgiveness.

At precisely eight o'clock, on the morning of 19th December 1934 Thomas Pierrepoint entered the condemned cell of 43-year-old Ethel Lillie Major and without a word pinioned her arms to her sides. Accompanied by her prison guards and with her executioner leading the way, she stepped towards the gallows which would momentarily and painlessly relieve her of her own life, unlike the way in which her husband had spent his final few moments on this earth.

12. THE CALCULATING CARER

"NURSE" DOROTHEA WADDINGHAM

Convicted of murdering Louisa & Ada Baguley

Born sometime around 1900, Dorothea Waddingham appears to have been a woman that made the most of what little she had been given by nature and by life, but ultimately found herself undone by her own avarice.

Reported to be a relatively unattractive individual, with a long thin face and protruding teeth, she was obviously pleasing enough to at least two men by whom she was thought to have had five children. Her husband, Thomas Leech, was said to have been a good deal older than Waddingham when they married and he was later thought to have died as a result of contracting throat cancer, leaving her with a number of small children to care for alone.

Following her husbands death, she began a relationship with a man closer to her own age, Ronald Sullivan and together the were said to have established a private unregistered nursing home at 32 Devon Drive in Sherwood in 1935. Although neither one had any formal nursing qualifications, this did not appear to be an obstacle to their setting up the business and Waddingham quickly appointed herself as the matron of the new home, with Sullivan acting as a general orderly.

Despite not having undertaken or achieved any sort of formal nursing qualification, Waddingham did have some experience as an orderly herself, having been employed in that role at the Burton-on-Trent Workhouse Infirmary, but this obviously did not qualify her to appoint herself as a matron in her own nursing home. However, this lack of any credible experience or training does not appear to have been a hindrance, as far as the local authorities were concerned and it was reported that the home received official recognition from the local nursing associations within a short period.

Within weeks of the business being opened two relatives were said to have been recommended to the new nursing home by the local authorities. Ada Baguley was an 87-year-old bedridden invalid who was thought to be suffering from dementia and had a serious heart condition. Her 50-year-old daughter, Ada Louisa, who was said to suffer from some sort of creeping paralysis, accompanied her mother into the home.

Perhaps because the two women had a limited income and ostensibly to ensure their long-term care, Waddingham was reported to have made a private arrangement with Louisa, whereby the mother and daughter would be cared for until their deaths, provided that Louisa made a new will, leaving her estate worth around £1500 to Waddingham. Obviously the Baguley's solicitor saw no problem with this arrangement and in May 1935, Louisa was reported to have rewritten her will leaving her entire estate to the kindly "Nurse" Waddingham.

Within days of her daughter having signed this new will however, her mother Mrs Ada Baguley was thought to have died as the result of a brain haemorrhage, or a stroke, which given her age and health problems was extremely sad, but not totally unexpected. With no reason to suspect anything untoward and with the cause of death given as a stroke the old lady was simply laid to rest by her daughter and Louisa returned to the nursing home.

In the September of 1935, a few months after her mothers death, Louisa herself was said to have died suddenly, again having suffered a stroke, which was not quite so expected. However, it was only when Dorothea Waddingham contacted Nottingham's Health Officer, Dr Banks, asking him to approve the cremation of Louisa Baguley body that suspicions began to surface. She provided Dr Banks with a letter, purportedly written by Louisa, asking that her body be cremated and that her relatives not be informed of her death. Clearly this was a highly unusual request from anybody and Dr Banks was so concerned that he immediately arranged for a full post mortem to be carried out on Louisa Baguley's body.

The pathologist, Dr Lynch, soon confirmed Dr Banks' worst fears announcing that Louisa's body was found to contain unusual levels of morphine, which could not be accounted for. As a result of these findings the authorities informed the Police and arrangements were made for the body of Ada Baguley to be exhumed and an examination carried out on her remains. Once again, the pathologist found evidence of unusually high levels of morphine in the woman's body, making it clear that both mother and daughter's deaths were suspicious and certainly not as the result of natural causes.

On the 24th September 1935, Detective Inspector Pentland of Nottingham City Police was said to have visited the Waddingham nursing home to make enquiries into the deaths of the two women and soon became aware of a possible motive, as well as potential suspects for the two murders.

With sufficient evidence to support a murder charge, the Police quickly arrested both Waddingham and her lover, Ronald Sullivan and charged them with the murders of Ada and Louisa Baguley after which they were remanded into custody.

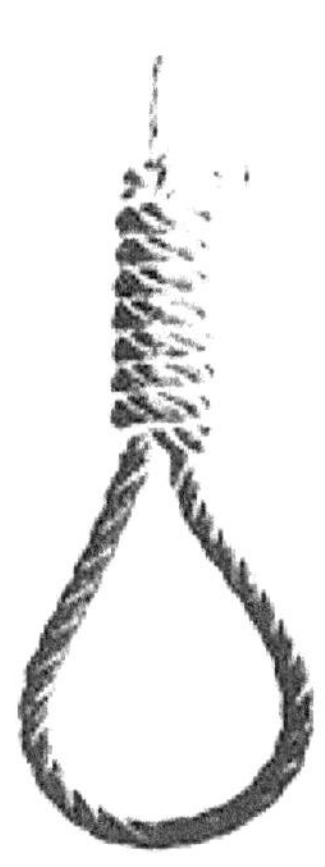

The pair were brought to trial before Mr Justice Goddard at Nottingham Assizes on 4th February 1936, but almost immediately it was announced that there was insufficient evidence to proceed against Sullivan and he was discharged by the court, leaving Waddingham to face the charges alone.

The "Nurse" tried to claim that the morphine had in fact been prescribed by the homes physician, Dr Mansfield, but he strenuously denied that he had ever ordered the drug for the Baguley ladies. He did recall however, that he had prescribed morphine for a former patient, a Mrs Kemp, but she had died in February 1935, so there could be little chance of "Nurse" Waddingham having got the patients or their medications confused.

Given the motivation of the Baguley estate she was due to inherit, her access to the drugs and the fatal doses of morphine found in the two women's bodies, it was clear to members of the jury that Dorothea Waddingham was entirely and solely responsible for the murders, simply to help support her family and her ailing business. Consequently, on the 27th February 1936 they found her guilty of the double homicide, yet surprisingly expressed a plea for mercy from the judge, something which neither he nor the Home Secretary felt bound to grant.

Sentenced to hang at Birmingham's Winsom Green Prison on the 16th April 1936, Waddingham still hoped to escape the executioner by claiming that she was pregnant and that the authorities could not kill her innocent unborn child. Although she was said to be still "nursing" her new 3-month-old baby boy in prison, a medical examination proved conclusively that she was not carrying a child and so the sentence could be carried out.

At eight o'clock in the morning of Friday 16th April 1936, Thomas Pierrepoint the official executioner, assisted by his nephew Albert stepped into the condemned cell at Winsom Green Prison and pinioned the 36-year-old mother of five before leading her to the gallows and sending her into eternity. It was later reported that just before her death, she had finally confessed to the murder of the two Baguley women.

13. THE INFATUATED WIFE

CHARLOTTE BRYANT

Convicted of murdering Frederic Bryant

Reported to have been born to a Roman Catholic family called McHugh in Londonderry about 1904, the young Charlotte McHugh was unfortunate enough to be born into a politically and religiously divided community that generally saw members of her own faith fail to prosper under what was still then an Ireland ruled by the British.

Whether it was choice or circumstance that caused her to become an illiterate good-time-girl who spent her later teenage years actively pursuing the British servicemen that were stationed in the city isn't clear, but her striking good looks and easy virtue were said to have certainly helped her to become a well known and popular figure in the pubs and bars of her home town.

It was almost certainly as a result of this lifestyle that she met Frederic Bryant, a serving soldier who was thought to be about eight years older than her and someone who could no doubt regale her with stories of his actions during the First World War. Perhaps he treated her better than the other soldiers did and was a little more understanding of her situation than she was used to, but it seems that for whatever the reason, she soon became attached to Frederic and the relationship blossomed.

With his service in the British Forces completed, Frederic was said to have returned home to England, with Charlotte accompanying him and within a short time they were thought to have settled down into a peaceful and happy married life together. Frederic found employment as a farm labourer at Wells in Somerset and while he toiled on the land, Charlotte was said to have stayed at home caring for their growing family. No doubt a simple man like Frederic considered his life to be relatively fulfilled, but that does not appear to have been the case for his wife, who was said to have found the solitude and isolation incompatible with her own basic nature.

Perhaps to replace the excitement and freedom that she had left behind in Londonderry, it was said that Charlotte soon began to have illicit affairs with a number of local men and in some cases charging them for her services. Although in a small community such secrets are hard to keep and people tend to gossip, when questioned about his wife's infidelity Frederic was reported to have been completely indifferent to her behaviour, even joking that at least her "work" brought extra money into the home.

It was probably because of her husband's indifference to her and their equally diminishing feelings for one another that finally caused Charlotte to allow someone else into her heart. He was Leonard Parsons, an itinerant horse trader who travelled around the country buying and selling livestock and who had probably met Charlotte as she went about her business of prostituting herself in one of the nearby towns or villages. Despite having a common law wife and several children himself, Parsons quickly fell into a serious relationship with Charlotte, which eventually resulted in him moving into the Bryant's tied cottage and occasionally sharing the marital bed with his lover while her husband slept in the same room as his children. Although this highly unusual and undoubtedly fraught relationship seems to have been accepted by all of the three parties involved, it was not seen as being usual or acceptable to Frederic's employers who were so outraged by the situation and the attendant gossip that they immediately sacked him from his labourer's post, forcing him to give up the cottage.

The Bryant's, their children and their lodger were soon thought to have relocated themselves to a new home, just outside Sherborne in Dorset, where Frederic found a new position as a farmhand. Initially things remained the same as before, but at some point after the move, Frederic seems to have fallen out with Parson's and ordered him to leave the house. The totally infatuated Charlotte left as well, but was reported to have returned home sometime later, ostensibly to smooth over the differences between the two men, which obviously she able to do, as Parsons was later thought to have resumed his role of "lodger".

However, not only did this prove to be a temporary arrangement, but also a turning point for Parsons in his relationship with Charlotte. Perhaps he began to sympathise for Frederic, felt pressured by Charlotte to marry her, or just simply began to tire of her, whatever the reason, it soon became clear that Parsons ardour was beginning to cool for the ageing and much more demanding Mrs Bryant.

Although it was never claimed that Leonard Parsons played any part in Frederic's death, it would have been interesting to know his thoughts when Frederic became ill in both May and August 1935 following meals made for him by Charlotte. Whether or not he suspected anything suspicious isn't clear, but within a few months of Frederic's illnesses Parson's was reported to have packed his bags and ended his relationship with her. Perhaps he had grown tired of Charlotte, whose fine looks were thought to have deteriorated over time, or possibly he was deliberately absenting himself from the house in order that he didn't come under any sort of suspicion in the event that the worst ever happened.

Charlotte was said to have taken Parson's departure very badly and was thought to have regularly sought him out in the surrounding pubs and bars, eager for him to return to her. Whether or not she blamed her husband for her lover's disappearance isn't known, but her subsequent actions would seem to suggest that she saw Frederic as being part of a problem that she was determined to resolve.

During one of her regular searches for Leonard Parsons around the local area, Charlotte was said to have met and befriended a widow woman called Ostler who had been left alone to raise a family of several young children. Maybe because her own relationship with Frederic was so poor, she was said to have invited Mrs Ostler and her children to come and stay with her own family at their cottage, a decision that certainly wouldn't have helped the Bryant's rescue their already strained marriage.

Within weeks of their new lodgers having moved in, Frederic was once again taken ill with severe stomach pains, which the local doctor simply diagnosed as a bout of gastro-enteritis, from which he eventually recovered. Around the 22nd December however, he had a reoccurrence of the problem and his condition was diagnosed as being so severe that he was immediately admitted to the local hospital where he subsequently died.

Given his occupation, the fact that he was a relatively fit, healthy man and had no history of serious illness his doctor was not only surprised but suspicious of his sudden death, so asked for an autopsy to be carried out on Frederic's body. Given his concerns, it probably came as little surprise when the pathologist reported back to him that he had found Arsenic in a number of tissue samples and that the death was obviously anything but natural. With his doubts confirmed the doctor immediately contacted the Dorset Constabulary who then sent officers to the Bryant house to begin a murder investigation.

As the Police had little evidence with which to charge anyone; and as Frederic was only a tenant at the cottage, the Police arranged for the whole household to be removed to the local workhouse where they could be cared for; and of course easily located, should they need to question them. A later search of the property revealed the burnt remains of a weed-killer container that had been placed in a stove, but later thrown out with the ashes. Enquiries in one of the surrounding towns revealed that the product, containing arsenic, had been purchased by a woman who had signed for it with a simple cross, presumably because she could not write her name. The shop assistants could not however remember what the woman looked like.

During their investigations the Police also became aware of the highly unusual nature of the earlier relationship between Charlotte and their former lodger, Leonard Parson and immediately set about locating the itinerant horse trader. He would later tell the authorities about his illicit love affair with Mrs Bryant, his dealings with her husband and the reasons for his ending the relationship, but it was his frank disclosure in open court detailing their sexual activities which ultimately proved to be so damaging for Charlotte, suggesting as it did that she was a highly immoral nymphomaniac who would go to any lengths to get what she wanted.

When the Police interviewed Charlottes new friend Mrs Ostler, she told them that Frederic was severely ill after taking a hot drink given to him by Charlotte and that Mrs Bryant had told her how much she hated her husband. The witness also claimed to have seen the weed-killer container in the house stove, prior to it being thrown out into the garden with the rest of the ashes, which was where the Police had subsequently found it.

At the same time that the Police were interviewing potential witnesses, they sent the burnt weed-killer container, along with a few items of clothing and some dust samples to their laboratories for testing. It would later transpire that there was evidence of the weed-killer in the house and in the pocket of an overcoat which it was later suggested had been worn by Charlotte when she purchased the weed-killer from the local shop. The fact that she was illiterate was also pointed out as being relevant, as the weeding agent had been signed for by a woman who marked the record with a cross, rather than a written name.

With what they believed to be a good case against her, the Police travelled to the workhouse where Charlotte and her children were staying and arrested her on suspicion of murdering her husband by poisoning him. She simply claimed that she was innocent of the charge and knew nothing about any poison.

Brought to trial at Dorset Assizes on Wednesday 27th May 1936, over the next few days Charlotte may well have been judged as much for her overtly immoral behaviour, as she was for her guilt in the death of her husband. Although there was little compelling direct evidence of her having killed Frederic, the accumulation of circumstantial evidence and the lack of any other credible suspect who may have wanted her husband dead, inevitably led the jury to one single conclusion, that Charlotte was indeed guilty of the crime. Although some concerns were expressed over her ability to follow the nuances of the trial, given her limited education, it seems that she was able to understand the proceedings and was reported to have given a good account of herself in the witness box. Sadly, this was not enough to convince the members of the jury that she was innocent of any wrongdoing.

On the final day of the trial and with all the evidence having been presented, the Judge summed up the case and reminded the jury that they had two simple questions to answer; was Frederic Bryant poisoned with arsenic; and was his wife Charlotte responsible for administering the arsenic? Clearly, the guidance offered by the judge helped to clarify the juror's deliberations and within an hour they had returned to the courtroom to announce that they had found her guilty of the charge.

With the verdict reached, the judge had little option but to impose the death sentence on the mother of five who stood in the dock before him, even though it was probably a punishment that was disagreed with by many in the court. Having received the judgement from the court, Charlotte was said to have stated that she was not guilty of the charge, before being taken down and transferred to Exeter Prison where the sentence was due to be carried out.

Almost immediately, the trial evidence, judgement and sentence were appealed by Charlottes counsel and her supporters who believed that the court had been misled by the evidence put before them, but it was all to no avail, as the authorities refused to stay the execution, stating that in their opinion there was no new substantive evidence which might overturn the jury's decision.

Consequently, at eight o'clock on the morning of Wednesday 15th July 1936 Thomas Pierrepoint and his assistant Thomas Phillips entered the condemned cell of 33-year-old Charlotte Bryant and quickly pinioned her arms to her side. Leading her the short distance to the gallows and placing her in the centre of the trapdoor, Phillips pinioned her legs, while Pierrepoint placed the white hood over her head, before placing the noose around her neck. Both men having stepped back, Pierrepoint released the retaining bolt and pulled the lever that dropped Charlotte into the waiting void below the scaffold.

An hour later, her body was gently lowered down and prepared for the necessary autopsy which would later reveal that her death had been instantaneous. With all of the necessary procedures completed, Charlotte's remains were later interred within the prison grounds. The Roman Catholic priest who had attended her in the final weeks of her life would later relate how she had met her fate with great stoicism, but without ever having admitted to the murder of her husband? It was also reported that the five orphaned Bryant children were later placed in the care of the local authorities, to be brought up by the state, with nothing else known about their fate or whereabouts.

14. THE MOST HATED CAMP GUARD

ELIZABETH VOLKENRATH

Convicted of War Crimes at Auschwitz & Belsen concentration camps

Elizabeth Volkenrath was born on 5th September 1919 at Schonau in the Silesia region of Germany. Although little is known of her early life, she was perhaps a typical product of a generation brought up on the rhetoric and teachings of Hitler's Nazi regime that first came to power when Volkenrath was only 14 years of age.

Up until 1939, she was known to have been employed as a hairdresser and following the outbreak of World War II was reported to have been reassigned to work in a munitions factory, helping to produce the arms that German troops would require in their war with Britain and her allies. She remained in this post until October 1941, when she was transferred to the SS Auxiliaries and sent to Ravensbruck concentration camp to train as a female guard, as part of the Nazi Party's emerging "Final Solution". The training at Ravensbruck was intense and Volkenrath, along with her fellow guards was instructed on how to treat prisoners, the rules and regulations governing their behaviour, as well as learning how to identify prisoner slowdowns and attempts at sabotage.

In March 1942 she was transferred to the Auschwitz-Birkenau concentration camp, working under another SS Auxiliary Johanna Langefeld, and was initially put in charge of a working party responsible for sewing. Although she admitted having attended selection parades at the camp, she defended herself by stating that she was there purely to supervise the prisoners and had no hand in actually choosing those who lived or died.

In December of the same year she was put in charge of Auschwitz-Birkenau Parcel Store, where Red Cross packages from relatives would arrive for those interned or imprisoned at Auschwitz. She was also said to have been in charge of the camp's bread store. At her trial in 1945, Volkenrath would state that she always made sure that the Red Cross parcels were delivered to inmates and those prisoners who worked with her in the stores would testify to that fact.

In September 1944, Volkenrath was moved to take charge of a working camp in Auschwitz No 1, which she claimed simply comprised a Cobblers shop and a Tailors shop and which according to her, was run entirely for the benefit of the prisoner inmates. It was during this period that she was accused of being involved in the murder of three prisoners who were hung at Auschwitz. Although it isn't entirely clear, this may relate to an incident where a number of prisoners were reported to have been involved with the deliberate destruction of one of the crematoria at the camp, an act that resulted in severe repercussions for those that were deemed to be involved. Although there is little definitive evidence that Volkenrath actually perpetrated the action herself, her role as Head Overseer in the Auschwitz-Birkenau camp from November 1944 to January 1945, would undoubtedly have called for her to be present at the executions.

In February 1945, as the camp at Auschwitz-Birkenau was being cleared by the Nazis, Volkenrath along with a number of other female guards was transferred to the Bergen-Belsen camp, where most of the inmate population were being sent, as a result of the Russian advances in the East. As soon as she arrived at her new posting, she claimed to have been hospitalised for a number of weeks and so took little part in the camp activities during that particular period. However, from March 1945, she was back at work and was reported to have been the senior female overseer in the Belsen camp, detailing duties to the other female guards and was by reputation "the most hated female guard in Belsen". This final posting was reported to have seen her share responsibility for the entire camp with her former Auschwitz colleague and SS contemporary, Irma Grese.

At the Belsen War Crimes trial, convened by the British military authorities from 17th September to 17th November 1945, Volkenrath and 43 other former concentration camp guards were all charged with contravening the terms of the Geneva Convention of 1929, regarding the treatment of prisoners. The trial was held at the courthouse at Luneberg in Germany and Volkenrath was defended by a serving British officer, Major Munro.

Quite apart from her general complicity in the deaths of thousands of prisoner inmates who died in the camps where she served, often from disease, beatings and starvation which was perpetrated by the camp guards as a group, Volkenrath was specifically identified by a number of former inmates as having committed individual acts of cruelty.

A Czech Jewess called Gertrude Diament testified that she had witnessed Volkenrath actively taking part in the selection of prisoners at Auschwitz during 1942 and that the female guard helped to load the condemned prisoners into Lorries, to be transported to the gas chambers.

Another witness, Etyl Eisenberg a Jewess from Belgium, testified that Volkenrath regularly came into her block to steal food and clothes from the prisoners. She related that the guard also had a habit of beating prisoners and pulling their hair, describing her as being very cruel.

A third witness, Alexandra Siwidowa, testified that she clearly recognised Volkenrath and that she was in charge of all the SS guards at the camp and beat many women prisoners across the head with a rubber truncheon. On a number of occasions she saw her beat women into unconsciousness.

Nettie Stoppelman, a Dutch Jewess said that Volkenrath made a habit of compelling female prisoners to "make sport", forcing them to run round fast and fall down and get up again, for anything up to an hour in the SS women's office. She also testified that she took away their cigarettes, clothes and bread.

In response to these accusations, Volkenrath stated that although she had indeed heard about the gas chambers from the prisoners, she had no direct knowledge of their whereabouts, although she admitted to having seen the crematoria from a distance. She strenuously denied that she had ever made selections, claiming that although she was present, it was the SS doctors who chose prisoners and not the guards. She was only aware that those chosen were sent to Block 25 and were never seen again.

Admitting freely that she was extremely strict with the prisoner inmates, Volkenrath vehemently denied any and all suggestions that she had personally murdered anyone. She had on occasion boxed prisoner's ears or slapped their faces, but this was always on the instructions of her superiors, Maria Mandel and Margot Dreschel and then only to prisoners who had done something wrong. She stated that the practice of "making sport" with female prisoners was entirely at the behest of Josef Kramer, the camp commandant; and was only done to punish inmates who had infringed camp rules, by having things in their possession that they shouldn't have had.

Volkenrath placed the blame for the many deaths at Belsen squarely on the shoulders of their superiors in Berlin, who kept sending more and more prisoners to the camp, despite being aware of the dire situation which was emerging at the camp. She also claimed that conditions were bad for all of those that were present at Belsen, both prisoners and guards alike. As for the conditions and the regime at Auschwitz, this she blamed on her immediate supervisors, Mandel and Dreschel, as well as Heinrich Himmler, the architect of the concentration camp scheme.

Despite the best efforts of her defence counsel and her refusal to admit any sort of complicity in the murder of thousands of prisoners, Volkenrath was found guilty by the British military tribunal and along with Irma Grese and Juana Bormann was sentenced to death by hanging. Following the sentence, she along with her former camp colleagues was transferred to Hameln Prison to await execution. It is interesting to note, that neither Volkenrath nor Bormann appealed for clemency against their death sentences, suggesting perhaps that both saw it as fair retribution for the acts that they themselves had perpetrated.

It seems clear that the three condemned female guards faced their impending doom with great bravery in the days prior to their deaths. The British executioner Albert Pierrepoint, who had to weigh and assess the women the day before their execution recalled;

Elisabeth Volkenrath was called. She, too, had made the selections for the gas-chambers. Apart from that, her general behaviour to the prisoners had made her, survivors said. the 'worst-hated woman in the camp'. I reflected that if she could top Irma Grese she must have been formidable. She was a good-looking woman. She did not flash the smile that Irma Grese had given, but she seemed steady, although nervous.

Whatever her state of mind was, it was reported that on the evening prior to their executions, Irma Grese, Juana Bormann and Elizabeth Volkenrath spent their final few hours together singing songs and drinking. Following her death on the morning of 13th December 1945, Elizabeth Volkenrath was placed in a simple wooden coffin and buried in the grounds of Hameln Prison.

It has been suggested by modern day mental health professionals that neither Elizabeth Volkenrath nor Juana Bormann were intrinsically bad or mad. Rather it has been claimed that both women were unfortunate enough to have the type of personality and mentality that could easily be manipulated by the political administration of Germany, along with those charged with running the Nazi concentration camp system.

15. THE BEAUTIFUL BEAST

IRMA GRESE

Convicted of War Crimes at Auschwitz & Belsen concentration camp

Of the 10 former female concentration camp guards executed by the British military after World War II, the youngest and reportedly one of the most notorious was Irma Grese, who has alternatively been dubbed the "beautiful beast" and the "angel of death" by a number of the women who had previously been held prisoner at the notorious Ravensbruck, Auschwitz-Birkenau and Bergen Belsen camps.

The title was well deserved for the strikingly handsome 22-year-old Grese, who with her Aryan good looks was the epitome of the German poster girl, with curly blonde hair, big blue eyes and pleasing countenance. It was hard for most reporters to reconcile the fact that the pretty young girl sitting in the dock, was in reality a monster who had helped to deliberately subject thousands of prisoners to inhumane treatment, brutal beatings, bitter starvation and ultimately to certain death.

She was born on October 7th 1923 at Wrechen, near Mecklenburg to an agricultural worker, Alfred Grese and his wife Bertha, one of five children that they would have together. Although little is known about Grese's early life, evidence given by her sister Helene to the British military tribunal in 1945, points to a young girl that was not academically gifted or particularly self confident and the loss of her mother through suicide in 1936, when she was just 13-years-old, would undoubtedly have been a shattering blow to the five young Grese children. It also became clear, from her sister's evidence that Irma, along with a generation of other German youngsters, had become totally enthralled by the teachings and ideology of the ruling Nazi Party, who advocated purity of the German race and the total eradication of the Jewish, Communist and Slavic influences that they believed had corrupted and undermined the former Weimar Republic and threatened their German way of life.

Although her father was known to have remarried, there is little evidence that Irma or her siblings were close to their father, or indeed to their new step-mother. At 15 years old Irma was reported to have left school, largely as a result of poor scholastic ability, an inability to fit in with her peers, which led to her being bullied and her preoccupation with the Nazi party, particularly the League of German Girls, a female youth organisation, of which her father strongly disapproved. Despite her poor academic qualifications, Irma still hoped to pursue a career in nursing, but found that the Labour Exchange would only offer her agricultural work, so for the next 6 months she was employed on a local farm, before she finally found a post working as a shop assistant in the town of Luchen.

Finally in 1939 she was offered a position as an apprentice Nurse's aid at the hospital in Hohenluchen, no doubt in the hope that she might gain the experience to train as a nurse, but instead she was to spend the next two years simply as a helper. However, her time at the hospital enabled her to make new and valuable contacts with the doctors and staff that worked there and it was thought to be one of these people that would ultimately set her on the road, which would inevitably lead to her career in the concentration camps. However, having left her hospital post in 1941 she was thought to have first drifted back into agricultural work, being employed as a dairy machine operator on a local farm.

Perhaps through one of her former colleagues at Hohenluchen Hospital, at the beginning of 1942 she was sent for a job as a guard at the nearby Ravensbruck prison camp, although Irma always denied that she went willingly, claiming that she had been conscripted into the work. Whatever the truth of her employment at Ravensbruck, as soon as her father found out he was said to have beaten his daughter and forbade her from returning to the family home. By the July of 1942 she was said to have completed her training at the camp and was officially employed as an "Aufseherin", becoming one of the youngest women in Germany to be employed in that particular role. It has been reported that Irma trained under another noted female overseer, Dorothea "Thea" Binz, who was reputed to be one of the most brutally sadistic women guards in any of the concentration camps and taught her new trainee guards to be exactly the same.

New female guards were taught to work alongside their SS male counterparts, as well as the officers and doctors who essentially ran the concentration camps. Although they were said to be equal to the male SS personnel of similar rank, it seems to have been clearly understood that no female could have direct control over a male SS guard. Rather, they were primarily employed to maintain order, help in the processing of prisoners, as well as administering the records of the camp.

During their training, female guards were warned against forming friendships or relationships with any of the prisoners and would have been regarded as a major infringement of the rules laid down by the camp authorities. Aside from the fact that such friendships encouraged favouritism and bias, they also helped to undermine the idea that the prisoners held in the camp were, in the eyes of the Nazi regime little more than "Dreck"; worthless sub-human rubbish that could be utilized, before being disposed of. New female overseers were also taught how to identify and prevent deliberate work slowdowns or sabotage, as well as how to administer punishments to those that infringed the camp rules.

Within a relatively short time, Irma was reported to be in a position of authority within the camp and helping to train the new and growing number of female guards who had been specially recruited to help implement the Nazi Party's "Final Solution".

By March 1943 Irma had made such a name for herself at Ravensbruck and had so impressed her superiors with her zeal and brutality that she was then transferred to the concentration camp at Auschwitz-Birkenau. Initially she claimed to have been employed as a telephone operator, commander of a gardening detail and finally as a mail censor. Within a relatively short time though, she had brought herself to the attention of the camp authorities and by the end of 1943 had been promoted to Senior Supervisor, the second highest female rank in the camp and directly responsible for the lives of over 30,000 women who were held in Camp C. It was during this period that she was said to have been responsible for selecting prisoners for the gas chambers, working alongside the notorious camp Doctor Josef Mengele, who was said to have been one of Irma's many lovers. During these selections she was accused of having personally chosen prisoners who were deemed to be too elderly, young or infirm to be employed in the camp's work programmes and consequently were sent to the gas chambers.

In January 1945 she was temporarily transferred back to Ravensbruck for a few weeks before being assigned to the Bergen Belsen camp in March of the same year. She was appointed as the Labour Control Officer, working under the camp commandant Josef Kramer, who was known as the "Beast of Belsen" because of his brutality towards the prisoners. This was to be Irma's final posting, as she was arrested by British troops when they liberated the camp in April 1945.

Along with 43 other concentration camp staff members, Irma was tried by a British military tribunal, convened under a Royal Warrant of 14th July 1945 which sat between September 17th 1945 and November 17th 1945. The charges laid against Irma and her former colleagues were derived from the Geneva Convention of 1929, regarding the treatment of prisoners, particularly the treatment of allied nationals who were named in the indictment. The Belsen War Crimes trial, as it was termed, was held at Luneberg, Germany where Irma was defended by a British officer, Major L S W Cranfield, a member of the Honourable Household Horse Artillery.

During her trial former female prisoners from Ravensbruck, Auschwitz-Birkenau and Bergen Belsen appeared for the prosecution and publicly detailed the atrocities that Irma was said to be responsible for. They accused her of numerous crimes, including the arbitrary shooting of prisoners, taking part in the selection of prisoners, which resulted in thousands of men, women and children being sent to the Gas Chambers; regular beating of camp inmates and using a half starved, attack trained guard dog to savage prisoners. Additionally, it was claimed that Irma regularly used both physical and emotional abuse to intimidate, harass and injure prisoners purely for her own perverted sexual pleasure.

Throughout her career in the camps, Irma was renowned for her immaculate appearance, including her beautifully tailored uniforms, a silver plated pistol that she wore around her waist and her lightweight transparent cellophane whip, which she was said to have had specially made in one of the camps weaving factories. In a deposition to the British authorities, she freely admitted to using the whip and a walking stick to beat prisoners whenever she felt it was necessary. She also admitted that due to its lightweight construction, the whip would hurt anyone that was struck with it.

It was stated by a number of the prosecution witnesses that Irma had regularly ordered non-German speaking prisoners to fetch items from outside of the compound wire, which would often lead to them being shot by the patrolling SS guards. One former prisoner even suggested that up to 30 prisoners a day would be killed in this fashion, although this seems highly unlikely.

A former prisoner from Auschwitz-Birkenau reported seeing Irma cold bloodedly shoot a female inmate dead, simply because she was standing outside of her assigned block when a new transport of prisoners was arriving at the camp, something which was against the rules. According to the witness, she had used a mirror to determine whether or not the shot woman was dead and the fact that the mirror didn't steam over when she held it near the shot inmate's mouth, told her that she was indeed dead.

A second female inmate from Auschwitz-Birkenau recalled an incident where two prisoners, a mother and daughter were talking to one another through the barbed wire which separated their prison compounds. Grese, who happened to be passing by on her bicycle spotted the pair talking and rode over to where they were standing, got off her bike and began to beat the mother with a leather belt. After the older woman had fell to the floor under the weight of the attack, Grese was reported to have continued kicking her with her heavy jackboots. The witness then testified that the injured woman had taken several weeks to recover from the beating and had been hospitalised because of it.

Another woman who had been a prisoner at Auschwitz related the story of two young female inmates who tried to escape by way of a barrack block window, but who had been caught and shot by Irma, as they lay on the ground outside the block.

Yet another prisoner told the tribunal about the case of an unnamed Hungarian woman who had been selected for the gas chamber and who then tried to hide away in a group who hadn't been chosen. The witness then stated that Grese, who had seen the woman's attempt to escape, reported the woman to a male SS guard who was standing nearby, who promptly turned around and shot the woman dead. The witness had not heard Grese instruct the guard to shoot the woman, but had formed the opinion that it was Grese's intervention that had directly led to the woman's death.

It was also alleged by a number of former prisoners, that Irma had used her position to sexually abuse female inmates, including raping them, indulging in homosexual activities and causing serious physical injuries to others, so that she could gain sexual satisfaction from watching them being treated for their wounds without the use of anaesthetic. It was also suggested by her accusers, that a number of the women who had been attacked by Irma were subsequently killed in order to stop them reporting her to the camp authorities, because such sexual activities were strictly forbidden under German law.

Following her capture at Belsen and her subsequent interrogation by the British authorities, she was asked to account for her actions and behaviour, Irma simply replied "Himmler is responsible for all that happened, but I suppose that I have as much guilt as do those above me"

Although she quite willingly accepted that she had been guilty of mistreating prisoners, in her own defence statement Irma had admitted carrying both a whip and stick, with which to beat prisoners, but she refuted any suggestion that she had killed anyone with them. She admitted attending the regular selection parades, but only to supervise the women prisoners and not to choose who would live or die. She stated that her duties called for her to attend such selections, which were run entirely by the political division of the camp and overseen by the camp's doctors, but her job was simply to keep a tally of the prisoners coming in and out of the camp. Although she agreed that she knew about the existence of the gas chambers, she claimed that this information had come from the prisoners themselves and was not something she was aware of from the beginning of her service.

She further admitted to beating inmates that tried to run away from or avoid the selections and then dragging them back to the inspection parades. She vehemently denied the charge that she had cold bloodedly shot any inmate, particularly the two female prisoners who were reported to have tried to escape through a barrack block window. This denial was supported by a second defence witness who stated that the block windows could not be opened, so the story of the two young women climbing through it to escape couldn't possibly be true.

At the end of her trial and with the death sentence having been handed down, Irma along with all but 2 of the condemned camp guards were reported to have appealed their death sentences to Field Marshal Montgomery, the British military commander. Needless to say the pleas for clemency were turned down in every instance.

With the sentences confirmed, those due to be hanged were returned to Hameln Prison, the town which is famed for the story of the Pied Piper. The unusual gallows which were specially built by the Royal Engineers within the prison was constructed with a double trap door, so that the male prisoners could be hanged in pairs, unlike the three female prisoners, who were executed individually.

Britain's official executioner Albert Pierrepoint was appointed and flown in to carry out the sentences, the first of 200 that he would be asked to officiate at. For some reason that has never been fully explained Pierrepoint was not allocated an experienced assistant for the executions so a member of the British Forces, Regimental Sergeant Major O'Neil was detailed for the task and would go on to assist in many of the other subsequent judicial executions of Nazi war criminals undertaken by the British authorities.

On arriving at Hameln Prison, Pierrepoint was dismayed to realise that the condemned prisoners would be able to hear their graves being dug in the prison yard outside their cells. When he made mention of it though, he was simply told that the noise was unavoidable, given the frozen conditions of the ground outside. Despite the onerous nature of his work, or the crimes of which the accused had been convicted, Pierrepoint saw it as part of his job to treat the condemned prisoners with the greatest care and respect, aware that he was the last human being that they would see prior to their death. In his later autobiography, Albert Pierrepoint would recall;

At last we finished noting the details of the ten men, RSM O'Neil ordered 'Bring out Irma Grese.' She walked out of her cell and came towards us laughing. She seemed as bonny a girl as one could ever wish to meet. She answered O'Neil's questions, but when he asked her age she paused and smiled. I found that we were both smiling with her, as if we realized the conventional embarrassment of a woman revealing her age. Eventually she said 'twenty-one,' which we knew to be correct. This blonde girl of twenty-one. who habitually carried a riding whip to lash prisoners to death, had, it was stated by one of her fellow-guards in the camp, been responsible for at least thirty deaths a day. O'Neil asked her to step on to the scales. 'Schnell!' she said — 'Quick, get it over.'

Having weighed and assessed the prisoners, once again Pierrepoint's humanity and consideration was reported to have shown through. Recognising her youth and the fact that all of the other prisoners would be able to hear their former comrades being executed, in order to spare Irma the ordeal of having to wait, he decided that she would be the first of the three women to hang. He remembered;

"The following morning we climbed the stairs to the cells where the condemned were waiting. A German officer at the door leading to the corridor flung open the door and we filed past the row of faces and into the execution chamber. The officers stood at attention. Brigadier Paton-Walsh stood with his wristwatch raised. He gave me the signal, and a sigh of released breath was audible in the chamber, I walked into the corridor. 'Irma Grese, I called.

The German guards quickly closed all grills on twelve of the inspection holes and opened one door. Irma Grese stepped out. The cell was far too small for me to go inside, and I had to pinion her in the corridor. 'Follow me,' I said in English, and O'Neil repeated the order in German. At 9.34 a.m. she walked into the execution chamber, gazed for a moment at the officials standing round it, then walked on to the centre of the trap, where I had made a chalk mark. She stood on this mark very firmly, and as I placed the white cap over her hand she said in her languid voice 'Schnell'. The drop crashed down, and the doctor followed me into the pit and pronounced her dead. After twenty minutes the body was taken down and placed in a coffin ready for burial."

Perhaps one of the most outlandish claims made against her, was that Irma had lampshades made from human skin, derived from the victims of the concentration camps and that she kept these items as trophy's from which she gained some sort of ghoulish pleasure. Other later sources however, have dismissed these claims, stating that in fact these lampshades were actually made from goatskins and not from the remains of former camp inmates.

In the post war years Irma has become a cult figure for many far right groups, not simply because of her political beliefs, but mainly because of her stoicism in facing her own early death. Unlike some, she did not run away, or simply blame her superiors, but genuinely seems to have accepted that she was personally responsible to some degree for the acts that she undoubtedly committed.

Later mental health experts have simply concluded that Irma's behaviour points to someone who was or who became a psychopathic sadist who lacked the ability to empathise with those around her and who was unable to form any sort of meaningful relationship with either men or women. The only way she could gain any sort of fulfilment was by means of the sexual gratification she derived from causing pain or degradation from those that were under her control.

Modern day experiments involving seemingly fair, well balanced and friendly individuals, both male and female, have proved that almost anyone can have their moral compass and their very humanity altered by certain circumstances. The old adage of *power corrupting* and *absolute power, corrupting absolutely* would appear to have some relevance in the case of several Nazi concentration guards, who were effectively given the power of life over death.

16. THE WOMAN WITH THE DOGS

JUANA BORMANN

Convicted of War Crimes at Auschwitz & Belsen concentration camps

According to her own evidence, given to the British military tribunal convened in 1945, to investigate war crimes committed at Bergen Belsen concentration camp, Bormann was born on 10th September 1893, at Birkenfelde in East Prussia. This was at odds with the widely accepted information, that she had been born in 1903 and was 42 years of age when she was brought to trial, when in fact she appears to have been ten years older than was generally assumed. Which of these two dates is actually her correct date of birth is unclear, but if she hoped that a greater age might help her to avoid punishment for her crimes, then she was tragically mistaken.

Along with many of her contemporaries who served with her in the SS Auxiliary, prior to her service in the concentration camps Bormann appears to have been an unremarkable individual, who was poorly educated, lacked self confidence and had been employed in a variety of unskilled and badly paid jobs. By her own admission, she had first joined the SS Auxiliaries as a civilian worker at the Lichtenburg concentration camp in 1938, ostensibly to earn more money. Prior to this she had been employed as a worker in a Lunatic Asylum, where she had received a fairly low monthly salary, so the prospect of earning three or four times as much money with the SS appealed to her.

Lichtenburg concentration camp was one of the first in Germany and was reported to have been in operation between 1933 and 1939, centred on a medieval castle complex. From 1933 until 1937 it was said to have held male prisoners, but from 1937 through to 1939 it held female internees only.

At Lichtenburg she was said to have worked under another SS Auxiliary Jane Berginau and was initially employed in the camps kitchens. However, in 1939 Bormann was reported to have been assigned as a female overseer for a working party which was helping to construct the new and emerging Ravensbruck concentration camp. Almost all of the staff from Lichtenburg was reported to have been transferred to Ravensbruck by May of 1939 and Bormann was said to have remained there until 1942.

In March of that year, she was transferred to the main Auschwitz camp, before being reassigned to the Auschwitz-Birkenau complex in the October of 1942. Her supervisors at the camp included the likes of Maria Mandel, Margot Drechler and the young Irma Grese, all of whom were notorious for their treatment of the prisoner inmates.

In 1944 Bormann was transferred yet again, this time to a satellite camp at Hindenburg In Silesia, but by the January of 1945 she had been returned to Ravensbruck, before finally receiving her last posting to Bergen Belsen, where she was reunited with her former colleagues from Ravensbruck and Auschwitz, Josef Kramer, Irma Grese and Elizabeth Volkenrath. Along with all the other camp guards at Belsen, Bormann was arrested by the British army when they liberated the camp in April 1945.

As part of the Belsen War Crimes Trial, several former prisoner inmates at both Auschwitz and Belsen testified against Bormann, including Anita Lasker, who remembered her, the fact that she had a dog with her and that almost all the prisoners feared her. The witness did say however, that she had never seen Bormann do anything untoward and she had never had any reason to complain about her.

Other witnesses had far less favourable recollections of the "woman with the dogs", including a former inmate called Esther Wolgruth who testified that she had seen Bormann set her dog on a Polish woman who had a bad leg and couldn't keep up with the main workgroup. She reported that the dog had badly mauled the injured prisoner, to the extent that the inmate subsequently died from her injuries.

A Czech Jewess called Vera Fischer testified that Bormann had been in charge of a female working party at Auschwitz and she was always accompanied by a large dog, which she used to attack weak or injured members of the workgroup. She claimed that a number of the women bitten by the dog went on to develop blood poisoning from which they died.

Alegre Kalderon another former prisoner claimed that she had personally witnessed Bormann commit brutal and savage assaults on a number of inmates that were in her charge. Rachela Kelisek, a Polish Jewess testified that in the summer of 1944 she had witnessed Bormann set her dog on a young girl called Regina, who was savagely mauled by the animal. The injured girl was said to have been hospitalised for blood poisoning and when Kalderon asked about her a fortnight later, she was told that Regina had died.

Perhaps one of the most damning witnesses against Bormann was a Polish woman called Yilka Malachovska who was a prisoner at Auschwitz in 1943. She testified that the former camp guard had been directly involved with the selection of prisoners from a working party of 150 inmates, one of whom was Malachovska's own sister. She stated that of the group, 50 were chosen and were forced into trucks which then took them to the gas chambers.

Anni Jonas, a Jewess from Breslau, who had been interned at Auschwitz, told the tribunal that she had witnessed Bormann attending selection parades and pointing individual prisoners out to the infamous Josef Mengele, telling him "this one looks quite weak".

Peter Makar, a Pole who was interned at Belsen told the court that he knew Bormann as the woman in charge of the pig-sties at the camp. He testified that in March 1945, he had personally witnessed Bormann beating inmates for stealing clothes and food. Additionally, he claimed that he had also seen Bormann and other female camp guards assaulting prisoners.

At her trial in Luneburg in 1945, Bormann admitted that she owned a dog while she was at Belsen, but strongly refuted any suggestion that she had used the animal to attack inmates, claiming that it was purely a pet and that it would have been a serious breach of camp rules for her to allow the dog to run round loose and attack prisoners.

She strenuously denied the claims made by a number of former prisoners from Auschwitz that she had participated in the selection of prisoners, simply claiming that she had only ever attended morning and evening roll-calls, as part of her regular camp duties.

At Belsen, she had been assigned to look after the camps pig-sties and admitted that she had slapped the faces and boxed the ears of prisoners who were cheeky or disobedient, but denied that she had severely beaten anyone. She was asked about the fact that the pigs were being fed, when thousands of prisoners were dying from starvation. Her answer to the court was simply "that she fed the pigs the food that was sent for them".

A large part of Bormann's defence was that former prisoners had mistaken her for another camp guard called "Kuck" who resembled her physically and who had also owned a dog at Auschwitz. Unfortunately for her, neither the court nor the British military authorities were able to find any record of a guard called "Kuck", leading them to believe that this was just a ploy by Bormann to absolve herself from any charges of wrongdoing.

When questioned by her defence counsel, Major Munro, Bormann testified that she had tried to resign from the SS Auxiliary in 1943, but that her request to leave had been turned down, even when her services were supposedly requested by one of Germany's vitally important materials suppliers.

She was also questioned about her behaviour and attitude towards the prisoners generally and whether or not she felt she had been too severe to them. Bormann simply replied "that she wanted to keep order", suggesting perhaps that she was prepared to do whatever was necessary to achieve that aim.

At the end of the Belsen Trial, Bormann, along with Elizabeth Volkenrath and Irma Grese was handed down a death sentence by the military tribunal, but unlike her former supervisor Grese, she along with Volkenrath did not plead for clemency from Field Marshal Montgomery, seeming to quietly accept the sentence handed down to her.

On the night before her execution, Bormann, along with Grese and Volkenrath were reported to have sung songs and drank together. Earlier in the day, Britain's official executioner, Albert Pierrepoint had weighed and assessed all the condemned prisoners and later noted in his autobiography;

Elizabeth Volkenrath was followed by Juana Bormann, 'the woman with the dogs', who had habitually set her wolfhounds on prisoners to tear them to pieces She limped down the corridor looking old and haggard. She was forty-two years old, only a little over five feet high, and she had the weight of a child, a hundred and one pounds. She was trembling as we put her on the scale. In German she said 'I have my feelings.'

At 10.38 on Friday 13th December 1945 Juana Bormann was hung at Hameln Prison in Germany and after her body had stayed there for twenty minutes, she was placed in a simple wooden coffin and her body buried in the grounds of the prison.

The overriding impression of Juana Bormann is of a slightly sad, weak individual who was destined to fail in whatever role she chose. The fact that she was part of a group which had absolute control over the lives of the inmates and yet still required a large dog to reinforce her authority would seem to point to a woman with little self confidence or indeed personal character.

17. THE MONSTER IN THE BUNKER

DOROTHEA "THEA" BINZ

Convicted of War Crimes at Ravensbruck Concentration Camp

Of the 3500 or so female camp guards that were employed as SS Auxiliaries, many of them were reportedly trained by Dorothea Binz and her cohorts at the infamous Ravensbruck Concentration Camp in Germany. Located some 50 miles north of Berlin, the prison camp at the "bridge of the Ravens" had first been constructed between November 1938 and May 1939, ostensibly to house German born female inmates whose activities were deemed by the new Nazi regime to be either criminal or anti-social. Women prisoners from two other camps, Sachsenhausen and Lichtenburg, were reported to have been forced to help in the construction of Ravensbruck's buildings, including the inmate barracks, camp kitchens and the main punishment block and jail, which later became known as the bunker.

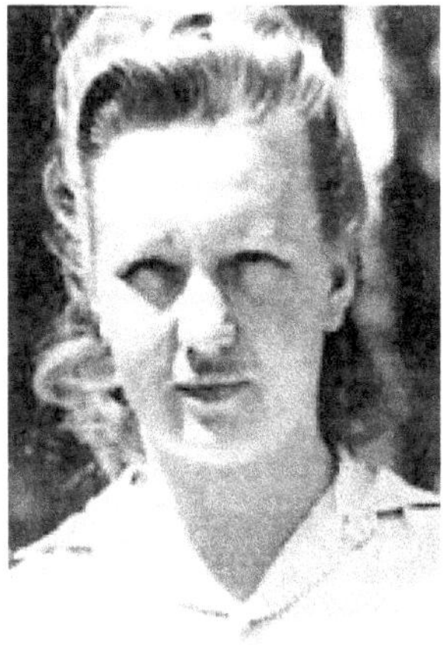

Once the internal buildings had been constructed, the whole camp area was then surrounded by high barbed and electrified wire fences, which carried a lethal enough charge to prohibit most prisoner escapes and was in addition to the ranks of armed male SS guards who patrolled the site accompanied by their highly trained and extremely vicious guard dogs.

Born on 16th March 1920 to a middle class German family, her father was reported to be a forester in the village of Alt Globsow near Furstenberg, Dorothea "Thea" Binz shared many similarities with her equally infamous compatriots, Irma Grece, Elisabeth Volkenrath, etc. In common with many of these young women, she was thought to be poorly educated and highly susceptible to the propaganda and rhetoric of Hitler's National Socialists party, who through organisations such as the League of German Girls, sought to indoctrinate the nations youth with their own distorted political beliefs and creed.

Having left school at 15 years of age in around 1935, Dorothea was said to have found employment as a housemaid to a local well-to-do family, a post that required little education, no great skill and by inference, offered little by way of reward. Finally in 1939, having turned 18 and no longer requiring her parent's permission to join, she was said to have applied for a training post with her local SS office, who could no doubt offer her the opportunities she so desperately sought and at the same time pay her twice the money she had previously earned.

Sent to the brand new Ravensbruck concentration camp for training, she soon adapted to life there and was thought to have been influenced and tutored by the likes of Emma Zimmer, Johanna Langefeldt and Maria Mandel, three of the most brutal female SS Auxiliaries employed within the camp system. Whether or not she was simply resentful and malicious to begin with is unclear, however it soon became clear to the authorities at Ravensbruck that the young Dorothea Binz had the characteristics that they wanted in their female guards and her vindictive, sadistic nature was not only approved of but actively encouraged in others.

With the purpose of the camp having fundamentally changed following the outbreak of war in 1939, although Ravensbruck remained an almost wholly female camp, instead of it being simply a prison, it became a transiting centre, a work camp, as well as a prison. Those women that were deemed to be a threat to the Nazi regime, regardless of their country of origin, were transported there to be processed and or utilised by the German government, as they saw fit. Jewish women were gathered there to be forwarded to the extermination centres like Auschwitz-Birkenau, communist and preacher alike were exploited by the ruthless industrial giants who fed and maintained the German military machine that was engulfing much of Europe and the camp even became the final destination for the many heroines who had found the courage to physically oppose the German invasion of their homelands.

For Dorothea Binz, having already worked within the camp's kitchen and laundry, the expansion of the Ravensbruck site and the demand for even more female guards, helped her to climb the promotional ladder within the camp. As new camps were opened throughout Europe, experienced female guards such as Maria Mandel, Johanna Langefeldt and Emma Zimmer were transferred away from Ravensbruck, leaving Dorothea Binz and others to be promoted in their stead.

By the August of 1943, she was recorded to have been appointed as the Deputy Chief Wardress to Greta Boesel and was said to be a pivotal member of Ravensbruck's command staff, responsible for the induction and training of new female warders. She was undoubtedly chosen for that role because of her unyielding abuse of the camps inmates, who she was accused of beating, slapping, kicking, and whipping at every opportunity. Several thousand new female guards were thought to have received training from Dorothea Binz and her staff, including the notorious Irma Grese, Elisabeth Volkenrath and the murderous Ruth Closius.

Although there were thought to be hundreds of incidents where "La Binz", as the French prisoners called her, was said to have killed or injured inmates one of the most atrocious was said to have taken place outside the camp and involved a female Polish prisoner. According to witnesses, Binz happened to be cycling past a wood cutting party when she noticed a prisoner not working as hard as she would have liked. Stopping the bike, the German guard dismounted and took hold of a pickaxe and started to beat the prisoner until she was little more than a bloodied mess. With the inmate lying dead or dying at her feet, Binz then proceeded to clean the blood off her boots using a piece of the prisoners uniform, before remounting her bicycle and continuing on with her journey.

It was no doubt because of such instances or at least the tales of such unprovoked attacks that made Dorothea Binz such a feared figure at Ravensbruck, leading to virtually all female inmates avoiding her presence if not her gaze. It was legendary amongst prisoners, that during both prisoner counts and selection parades, as soon as Binz arrived, silence fell amongst the prisoners; such was her wrath if she caught someone talking during either. Patrolling the camp with a whip in one hand and a vicious German Shepherd Dog in the other, she was said to have spent a great deal of time looking for those that broke camp rules or who were slacking from their assigned tasks.

Her rise up the promotional ladder and her utter contempt for the prisoners may both have been the result of her relationship with an SS Officer called Edmund Brauning who she was said to have shared a home with at Ravensbruck. The couple were reputed to have taken romantic walks together around the camp, watching and laughing as prisoners were beaten and humiliated by their SS comrades, before walking on to find some other event that would entertain them further.

In addition to her training duties, Binz was also reported to have been in day-to-day charge of the camp's jail and detention centre, which was commonly known as the "Bunker". Consisting of 78 small airless cells located on two separate floors, each room was empty, save for a folding plank of wood which served as both bed and bench. Female prisoners could be sent to the bunker for the most minor offences, including not making their bunk properly or wearing non-uniform items of clothing and might spend weeks or months in the onerous confines of the jail.

Binz was said to have used the bunker as her personal pleasure ground, imprisoning and interrogating prisoners on a whim and using the tiny prison cells to hold women that she had taken against or who she believed were guilty of some real or imaginary wrongdoing. Occasionally they would simply use the jail and the bodies of the defenceless prisoners to refine their torture techniques, to learn how to hurt women in a specifically female way, both for their own interest and perhaps for their own insane pleasure. Specifically, Dorothea Binz was reputed to enjoy beating prisoners with whips and was even thought to have devised some sort of electric whip with which she could punish and inflict pain on her victims.

The Special Operations Executive agent "Odette" Sansom, who was betrayed to the Gestapo, recalling her months of confinement in the jail made special mention of the seemingly endless screaming that came from neighbouring cells and how it almost undermined her own reserves of courage as she lay waiting her own turn. Fortunately for her, her assumed surname of Churchill and the cowardly self interest of Ravensbruck's commandant Fritz Suhren helped to protect her from the murderous attention of the female camp guards that frequently inhabited the bunker.

Although there was no static gas chamber at Ravensbruck until around February 1945, when one was finally built on the orders of Heinrich Himmler, the camp and its staff were known to have taken a full and active part in the Nazi Party's pre-planned extermination of Europe's Jews, otherwise called the "Final Solution". However, prior to the construction of the gas chamber at Ravensbruck the policy was implemented through cruelty, starvation, disease and where necessary, with a bullet.

Selection parades always took place, either for prisoners to be transported to the gas chambers, to the prison hospital for experimentation or to the nearby woods where thousands were shot and then burnt in huge pits or the camps later crematoriums. Regardless of the method, the choice of who was to die and who was to live was a lottery, determined by individual SS Officers, Doctors and the female guards themselves.

The fact that Dorothea Binz and her cohorts chose prisoners to die is indisputable, as is the fact that their cruelty and depravity caused thousands to perish as the result of starvation, beatings, disease and exhaustion that they themselves, either individually or as a group, had caused. Over the period of nearly six years, between its opening in May 1939 and its liberation by the Russian Army in the spring of 1945 it has been suggested by some sources that over 90,000 men, women and children had perished at Ravensbruck

Along with many of her SS colleagues, on the 27th April 1945, a day or so before the camp finally fell to the Russian Army, up to 20,000 prisoners who were thought fit enough to walk were evacuated from Ravensbrook by their guards, including Dorothea Binz, who was said to be riding her bicycle westward, towards the British and American armies that were occupying her country. Perhaps, along with many others, during that final death march, she too decided to dispose of her uniform, her camp identity, as well as the thousands of human beings that they had tried so hard to destroy. Whatever, Thea Binz did during those subsequent hours isn't known, but it was later reported that a Russian scout unit finally caught up with and liberated the remaining Ravensbrook prisoners, finally releasing them from years of horror and cruelty.

Within weeks of the camp having been liberated, a number of the camp's former SS guards had been identified, found and arrested, including Dorothea Binz who was arrested by the British military on 3rd May 1945. Following her capture, she along with a number of other SS auxiliaries was taken to a newly established prison at Recklinghausen, on a site formerly used as a satellite for the infamous Buchenwald concentration camp.

Binz was finally brought to trial at the first Ravensbruck War Crimes Trial established by the British Military Authorities in Hamburg and held between 5th December 1946 and 3rd February 1947. All of the accused were charged jointly with *"committing a war crime in that they, at Ravensbruck in the years 1939-1945 when members of the staff of Ravensbruck Concentration Camp in violation of the laws and usages of war were concerned in the ill-treatment and killing of Allied nationals interned therein."*

After an eight week trial, during which former prisoners, including the former SOE agent Odette Sansom gave dramatic and blood-chilling testimony as to their experiences at Ravensbruck and the actions of the SS staff who stood in the dock, Dorothea Binz, along with Elisabeth Marschall, Greta Boesel and Vera Salvequart were all sentenced to hang for their crimes.

At nine o'clock in the morning, on the 2nd May 1947 Dorothea Binz faced the British executioner Albert Pierrepoint as she stood on the gallows at Hameln Prison, where some 16 months earlier three of her pupils, Irma Grese, Elisabeth Volkenrath and Juana Bormann had each faced their final few moments on earth. Whether the former Deputy Chief Wardress of Ravensbruck faced her end with the same stoicism as her late SS comrades is unknown, but certainly she was offered a far quicker and much more humane death, than she herself had offered to the hundreds, perhaps thousands of innocent women who she had helped to murder between 1939 and 1945.

18. THE HORRIFYING HEAD NURSE

ELISABETH MARSCHALL

Convicted of War Crimes at Ravensbruck Concentration Camp

Born sometime around 1886 in Germany, as Elisabeth Marschall took her final few steps to the British gallows which would ultimately end her life on the 2nd May 1947, she not only entered the history books as the oldest female Nazi concentration camp worker ever to be hung by Britain, but also joined the relatively small number of trained nurses who have gained worldwide recognition and everlasting condemnation for the cruelty and cold indifference that they showed to those who were seeking their pity and care.

Marschall was brought to trial at the first Ravensbruck War Crimes Trial established by the British Military Authorities in Hamburg and held between 5th December 1946 and 3rd February 1947. All of the accused were charged jointly with *"committing a war crime in that they, at Ravensbruck in the years 1939-1945 when members of the staff of Ravensbruck Concentration Camp in violation of the laws and usages of war were concerned in the ill- treatment and killing of Allied nationals interned therein."*

Thought to have qualified as a nurse in 1910, Marschall was said to have received her formal medical training at Meiningen, before finding employment at the Hermann Goering Works in Braunschweig. In 1931 and having become enraptured by the ideals and philosophy of the emerging National Socialist party led by Adolph Hitler, the 45-year-old nurse was reported to have willingly joined the Nazi party, later telling the allied authorities that she believed Hitler to be the only man who could save Germany from almost certain destruction.

Despite her membership of the ruling party, she was thought to have found herself being investigated and interrogated by the fearsome Gestapo, after she had been accused of secretly giving food to two French prisoners who were employed within the factory, thereby depriving her fellow Germans of much needed food supplies. As a result of her apparently unpatriotic generosity towards the two prisoners, Marschall was then said to have been forcibly transferred to the new Ravensbruck concentration camp, located north of Berlin and in common with many other German prison camps in desperate need of trained personnel.

Because of her specialist medical knowledge and experience the disgraced nurse was put to work in the camp's hospital and within a short period of time was said to been appointed as the Head Nurse or Oberschwester, the person who was in day-to-day charge of the ward orderlies and conscripted prisoner-nurses. It was a role that she was said to have relished, allowing her to play a full and uncompromising part in the Nazi party's "cleansing" of both their home nation and the countries of continental Europe that were unfortunate enough to fall under the influence of Hitler's National Socialist Party.

As part of their duties at Ravensbruck, Marschall and her medical colleagues were reported to have carried out inhumane experiments on prisoner inmates in the camp's hospital, personally selected individual patients for transportation to the death camp at Auschwitz and to have purposefully murdered individual patients by injecting them with a drug called "Luminal", a Phenobarbital which had been extensively used by Nazi physicians since the early 1930's. In large enough doses the drug was known to cause the patients central nervous system to shut-down which could then lead to pulmonary oedema or acute renal failure in the helpless prisoners. At her trial Marschall was directly accused of having personally murdered five Jewish women patients who she injected with "Luminal" one after the other. The final victim having witnessed the effect of the drug on her fellow inmates was reported to have tried to physically stop the Nazi nurse from administering the injection, but was so weak from illness and hunger that she was easily overcome by Marschall and died shortly afterwards.

The medical experiments conducted by Ravensbruck's doctors, assisted by Marschall and her cohorts were reported to have begun in the summer of 1942 and included deliberately infecting patients with gas gangrene and other bacterial infections to study the effects of Sulfonamide drugs on these typical "battlefield" wounds. The camp doctors and nurses were also said to have carried out experiments in bone and tissue transplantation from the hospital's Polish female inmates many of whom were left in excruciating pain before dying from their deliberately inflicted injuries, or otherwise being sent to the Auschwitz gas chambers in order to hide the full truth of the camp's medical atrocities.

Typically, pregnant Jewish female prisoners were sent straight to the gas chambers, whilst those non-Jewish women who were carrying unborn children had little chance of their infants surviving the rigours and hardships of Ravensbruck. Between 1942 and 1944 it was later reported that all newborn babies born in the camp's hospital were systematically strangled at birth by one or two of the prisoner nurses, with the full knowledge and connivance of Elisabeth Marschall and her superiors. The infants bodies were then said to have been disposed of in the camp's heating furnaces, thus allowing their grieving mothers to be forced back to work, without the perceived hindrance of a young child to worry about or look after. Even after 1944 when the Nazi authorities at Ravensbruck were said to have reversed this murderous policy on prisoner's children, most newborn infants continued to die from either starvation or disease, often because their mother's were to ill and weak themselves to breast feed their children and little or no additional nourishment being provided by the hospital's German staff.

Marschall herself was later accused of deliberately withholding vital Red Cross food parcels from her patients, many of which contained the supplies that were so desperately needed by these nursing mothers and their babies. In addition she was also said to have forced new mothers to leave their babies unattended and unfed while they were driven to work by whip wielding guards, often for the whole day and leaving the infants in the care of totally unsuitable and untrustworthy female inmates who had been specifically selected for the task by Nurse Marschall. On at least one occasion the Nazi medic was reported to have ordered that some 50 female prisoners and their babies should be loaded into a cattle truck without any food, water or milk. All were said to have subsequently died.

On another occasion Marschall was reported to have been directly involved with the selection of over 800 female prisoners who were later transported to Auschwitz, where most, if not all died in that extermination centre's gas chambers. It was later stated at the first Ravensbruck Trial, held by the victorious British military forces in Hamburg that Marschall was renowned for her daily review of the hospitals patient's records, when she was said to have selected those individuals who were to die and those that could live for another day. In fact, the nurse was thought to be a prolific record keeper and was said to have diligently recorded every birth, death and patient transfer within the camp's hospital, as well as helping to keep scrupulously accurate notes on many of the medical experiments performed there.

Prior to February 1945 prisoners at Ravensbruck were either shot, strangled, poisoned or simply beaten to death and their remains transported to the nearby Furstenberg Crematorium for disposal. However, from 1945 onward Ravensbruck was reported to have its own Crematoria, consisting of two ovens which were fully employed in hiding the evidence of the horrors that were taking place within the camp, including the disposal of the bodies of four female SOE agents who were killed there. Equally large numbers of Jewish prisoners were transported to Auschwitz-Birkenau, where they would continue to be exploited and mistreated, before being taken to the gas chambers which had been deliberately constructed for the specifically monstrous purpose of eradicating the non-Aryan races of Europe. From February 1945 onwards however, Ravensbruck was known to have had its own gas chamber, where in as little as a three month period, some 5,000 prisoners were known to have lost their lives, before the camp was finally liberated by Russian military forces in April 1945.

The trial also illustrated the contradictory nature of Elisabeth Marschall's nature, where she would employ her nursing and medical skills to their very best, notably when she was treating members of the camp's SS contingent who became ill at Ravensbruck. On occasion she was also known to have both mistreated and cared for different allied personnel who came into contact with her, the most notable case being Odette Sansom who was a member of the British Special Operations Executive. Odette had been sent to Ravensbruck ostensibly to be executed, but thanks to the selfish nature of the camp's commander and the successful advance of allied forces following the D-Day landings, she managed to survive the war. However, whilst she was being held in Ravensbruck's infamous "Bunker" she later recalled how she had become seriously ill and that it was Elisabeth Marschall, the Head Nurse of Ravensbruck who had come to her dimly lit cell to administer the treatment which ultimately saved her life.

Four other female SOE agents who were imprisoned at Ravensbruck were not so fortunate however, and the fact that Marschall herself may or may not have played any significant part in the deaths of Denise Bloch, Cecily Lefort, Lilian Rolfe and Violette Szabo, who were all executed at Ravensbruck, was relatively unimportant. The fact that she and her former SS comrades were deemed to have ill-treated and murdered allied nationals who were in their charge was sufficient grounds for the post war authorities to try them and in some cases to legitimately execute them. For Marschall personally, the fact that a trained nurse had allowed herself to commit horrendous acts against those that were in her care simply made matters worse and her death sentence perhaps even more inevitable.

Testifying in her own defence, Marschall claimed that many of the allegations made against her were entirely false and that in some cases she had been simply following orders given to her by her superiors. Most reporters concluded that the accused nurse deliberately played down her own role in the camp's hospital, by claiming that many of the atrocities were committed by the hospital's doctors and prisoner nurses, rather than by her. The accusation that she had murdered five Jewish patients by injecting them with Luminal was strongly rejected by the nurse, as was any suggestion that she had actively engaged or participated in the selection of prisoners for the gas chambers. Rather, she tried to convince the court that much of her time and efforts had been spent providing care and pain relief for those that were in her charge. She offered the court the following description of herself, *"I was not always nice, but when you think of the people who came into the camp and who did not always behave properly, then it is possible that I wasn't very nice. But all I can say is that I always listened to them and tried to be as fair as possible".*

19. THE ROTTEN CAMP GUARD

GRETA BOESEL

Convicted of War Crimes at Ravensbruck concentration camp

Born Greta Mueller on the 9th May 1908 at Elberfeld in Germany, Boesel was yet another trained nurse who found her way into the Nazi concentration camp system established by Hitler's National Socialist Party and who was reported to have played an active part in the mistreatment and murder of the female prison population.

Initially assigned to the Ravensbruck concentration camp for training, Boesel was reported to have remained there throughout the war, starting her career as an ordinary "Aufseherin" or wardress and later being promoted to the rank of Work Overseer. In common with most of her contemporaries, she was said to have shown nothing but utter contempt and cruelty to the prisoners in her care and her attitude to the sick and infirm was clear as she was heard to state "If a prisoner cannot work, then let them rot".

By November 1944 she was thought to be actively participating in the selection of prisoners who were to perish in the gas chambers of both Ravensbruck and Auschwitz-Birkenau, generally those deemed too old or sickly to continue slaving away in the industrial complexes of the Third Reich. Many of those chosen were invariably sent to the satellite camp at Uckermark, where their misery was continued and compounded until the day they would be loaded into sealed truck and poison gas canisters thrown in to murder the inmates, several hundreds at a time.

It was also in 1944 that Boesel was reported to have taken over the post of Report Overseer, a job that required her to administer the daily roll calls and oversee the general discipline of the prisoners within the camp. The roll calls were said to be tiresome and chaotic affairs, with tens of thousands of sickly, half-starved and extremely noisy inmates having to be counted and balanced against the camp records and any discrepancy accounted for. Often this daily routine would begin around five o'clock in the morning and last for several hours, with little consideration given to adverse weather conditions or the fact that the women faced at least twelve hours of hard labour in the coming day.

Whilst the female prisoners stood in rows to be counted, they were continually monitored by the SS guards who were assigned to watch them and who were only too happy to inflict pain and suffering on those inmates who disrupted or delayed the daily roll calls. Even seriously ill prisoners were required to attend these daily counts and there were hundreds of reported incidents where SS overseers would beat and bludgeon a sickly woman until she was finally forced outside to attend the block count, or simply died through her illness or mistreatment.

By March and April of 1945 it was becoming clear to Ravensbruck's command structure, including Greta Boesel that Russian forces would almost inevitably liberate the camp and so a decision was made to evacuate some 25,000 prisoners, who were destined to be marched to Mecklenburg, further inside the increasingly shrinking Reich. Unfortunately for many of the guards who remained, the Red Army finally liberated the camp on the 30th April and quickly exacted their own form of retribution on those that were brave or foolish enough to retain their SS uniforms, executing many and taking the remainder back to Russia to serve out the rest of their lives in Stalin's notoriously primitive Gulags.

Many of Ravensbruck's upper echelon survived however, by running westward towards the British and American forces that were now penetrating deep into the German homeland. The likes of Fritz Suhren, the commandant of the camp, along with many of the doctors and female guards, including Dorothea Binz, Emma Zimmer and Greta Boesel abandoned their uniforms, along with their Nazi ideology and attempted to survive the war under the protection of the western powers, rather than face the wrath of Russia's vengeful troops who were anxious to gain retribution for the millions of its citizens who had been so easily murdered by Hitler's armies.

Greta Boesel, having headed west with her comrades and her husband was eventually arrested by allied troops and handed over to the British military authorities while investigations were made into her actions at Ravensbruck. Along with other former wardresses, she was accused by a number of surviving inmates from the concentration camp of mistreating prisoners, murder and participating in the selection of women for the gas chambers.

She stood trial, along with Dorothea Binz, Vera Salvequart, Margaret Mewes, Elisabeth Marschall, Carmen Mory and Eugenia Von Skene at the first Ravensbruck War Crimes Trial which was held at the Curiohaus in Rotherbaum between 5th December 1946 and 3rd February 1947. Greta Boesel, along with Binz, Salvequart, Marschall and Mory all received a death sentence from the British court, although Carmen Mory a Swiss national found guilty of war crimes committed suicide before the sentence could be carried out. For three of the remaining four women, their executions were duly carried out on the 2nd and 3rd May 1947 at Hameln Prison by Albert Pierrepoint, following which their remains were buried in the precincts of the prison. The fourth woman, Vera Salvequart appealed her death sentence to the King, claiming that she had acted as an allied agent and had tried to smuggle secret Nazi plans for the V2 rockets to British authorities. Unfortunately for the Czech born nurse, the English monarch and his advisors ignored her appeal for clemency and she was subsequently executed on 2nd June 1947 at Hameln Prison by Pierrepoint. Margaret Mewes and Eugenia Von Skene, the other two women who had been tried at the same time were each sentenced to ten year prison terms and having served some four or five years in jail were then released.

20. THE KILLER PRISONER NURSE

VERA SALVEQUART

Convicted of War Crimes at Ravensbruck and Uckermark concentration camps

Born on the 26th November 1919 in Czechoslovakia Vera Salvequart was yet another trained nurse who was accused and found guilty of misusing both her vocational and professional skills by actively participating in the mass murder of women prisoners at Ravensbruck concentration camp and its associated extermination centre, which was known as Uckermark.

Having moved to Germany during the inter-war years, Salvequart was reported to have fallen foul of the Nazi states stringent racial laws which forbade intimate relationships between people of Germanic or Aryan descent and those deemed to be impure by the National Socialist leadership, including Jews. Salvequart was arrested for the first time in 1941 having been accused of conducting a relationship with a Jewish man and subsequently refusing to disclose his whereabouts to the Gestapo officers who interviewed her. As a result of her offences and undoubtedly because of her refusal to co-operate she was thought to have been sentenced to a 10 month jail term at Flossenberg.

Having served her sentence and been released back into German society, Salvequart was rearrested in 1942 for the same offence, conducting an illegal relationship with a Jewish man, although whether or not it was the same person who was involved in the first case is unclear. Found guilty of the charge yet again, this time Salvequart was sentenced to a two-year jail term, presumably in the same prison that she had so recently left.

Released yet again, the nurse was thought to have come to the attention of the Nazi authorities in the December of 1944 when she was arrested on suspicion of having helped five allied officers to escape capture, an offence which was regarded so seriously that she was sentenced to imprisonment at the female concentration camp at Ravensbruck, which by this time had become a death camp for most of the women that were incarcerated within its barbed wire fences.

Because of her status as a trained nurse and due to the shortage of trained personnel, as soon as Salvequart arrived at Ravensbruck she was assigned to the infirmary or "Revier" at the satellite camp known as Uckermark. This had originally been established as a prison camp in May 1942 for German girls, aged between 16 and 21, who were deemed to be either criminal or anti-social by the Nazi authorities and who were later transferred to the main camp at Ravensbruck, once they had turned 21.

From January 1945 the purpose of this "youth camp" was changed, becoming a centralised centre for the extermination of female prisoners who were classified as "unfit to work" by the Ravensbruck camp authorities or those women who were known to be over 52 years old. Prisoners sent to Uckermark were reported to have been brought to Salvequart's block and ordered to undress, while she and the camp's female guards determined who was to die immediately and those who would be spared for another day. Forced to stand for hours in freezing conditions and without any clothes, eventually those selected for death would be herded together and placed in a separate block to await their fate, while the remaining prisoners were allowed to dress and placed in grossly overcrowded, filthy barracks to await the next selection parade.

For those unfortunates who had been selected to die, evenings generally brought an end to their misery, when several trucks would be driven up to the doors of the barracks and they would be forced to crawl and scramble into these mobile gas chambers. Many were said to have pleaded and struggled for their lives, but always to no avail. Dragged, punched and kicked into the back of the vehicles, once they were full to capacity, the doors would be closed and the driver would throw a container of poison gas through a grill and then simply close it up again. Within minutes the shouting and banging would stop, any excess gas would be vented, and then the truck was driven away for the women's lifeless bodies to be disposed of.

Seemingly not content with playing her part in this merciless and macabre practice, Salvequart was also accused of personally murdering a number of patients by other means, a claim which she continued to deny throughout her later trial. According to some former inmates, the Czech nurse would regularly administer a white powder to sickly patients, all of whom would subsequently die within a short time. As rumours abounded amongst the prisoner body and more and more refused to ingest the powder, Salvequart was then reported to have become more direct in her methods and simply injected patients with Luminal or other noxious substances, in fact anything that would kill them quickly and more effectively.

She was also said to have filled out the death certificates for the murdered victims, often stating that the prisoner had died from pneumonia, heart failure, or some other such common ailment that could never be proved either way. Salvequart was also thought to be responsible for the removal of gold teeth and any other valuables that might have been secreted by the fated prisoner, all of which were supposedly used to help finance the Nazi's continuing war effort, but often ended up in the hands of greedy SS guards or camp administrators.

Speaking later at her trial which was held by the victorious British military authorities, Salvequart in response to the many allegations made against her stated; *"I remember that the sick did not trust me in the beginning, because they thought that I was part of the mass murder that was taking place. If I had been in their place, then I would have had the same impression. I was locked up, couldn't go anywhere alone and all that the prisoners knew about me, was that I lived where they murdered so many people.*

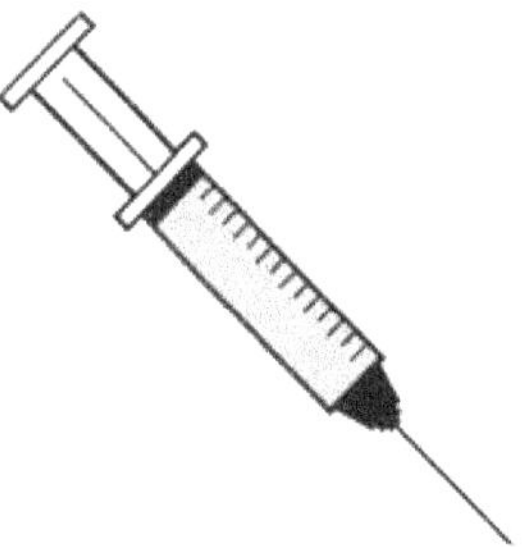

The accused nurse also told the court that she had always tried to do her best for her patients and on several occasions had saved selected prisoner's lives by switching their camp identification numbers with those that were already dead, essentially making them disappear from the camp's records. She further claimed to have saved the life of at least one baby, who might otherwise have been murdered in the hospital, by hiding him away and arranging for male prisoners to bring food and milk to feed the infant.

Because of the kindness that she allegedly showed prisoners, Salvequart claimed that she had put her own life in danger and towards the end, as the allies approached Ravensbruck, had been under threat of being sent to the gas chambers herself. It was only through the actions of several male inmates, who disguised her as a man, that she had managed to avoid being liquidated by the Nazi's and it was in this state of dress that she was finally discovered by American troops and immediately arrested.

Although she freely admitted the charge of having completed thousands of bogus death certificates, she had been forced to do so by her immediate superiors and if she had refused, then it was likely she too would have suffered a similar fate as the other unfortunate prisoner's and been sent to the gas chamber or simply shot.

As part of her defence, the Czech nurse also claimed to have been helping to steal information on the Nazi's vengeance weapon, the V2 rocket, which was said to have been produced near the camp until 1944. Salvequart stated that she had managed to get hold of plans for these fearsome weapons and was actively trying to smuggle them to the British whilst she was still a prisoner at Ravensbruck.

Despite her claims of innocence and the defence that she had been actively involved in espionage for the allied cause, the military court found the Czech nurse guilty of war crimes and sentenced her to die by hanging. Unlike some of the other camp guards, she did appeal her death sentence, but it served only to delay what was an almost inevitable end and on the morning of the 26th June 1947 in Hameln Prison, Vera Salvequart was executed by Britain's official executioner Albert Pierrepoint. The body of the 28-year-old was later interred in the grounds of the prison, along with the remains of the other camp guards who had been executed for their crimes against the people of Europe.

21. THE BOASTFUL KILLER

RUTH CLOSIUS-NEUDECK

Convicted of War Crimes at Ravensbruck and Uckermark concentration camps

Ruth Hartmann was born into an ethnic German family who lived in Breslau, Germany on the 5th July 1920 and although little is known about her early life, it is likely that she and her family were directly affected by the rise of Hitler's National Socialist Party, which not only sought to rebuild the country, but also to re-educate and control its native population. The young Ruth particularly would have been susceptible to the propaganda of the emerging Nazi Party, especially after 1933 when the party came to political power and the League of German Girls became an almost mandatory youth organisation for young female teenagers. Unlike the Hitler Youth which was aimed at boys and young men who could ultimately be diverted into the country's armed forces, the League of German Girls was designed to foster and support required Germanic and Aryan traits within the nation's young women, including beauty, health and ethnic purity.

As with all classes of the native German population, young and old, the dangers of foreign, ethnically unclean races, notably the Jews, was a major part of the Nazi re-education and propaganda program which was directed at the country's youth particularly. Both at school and during League summer camps, the likes of the teenage Ruth Hartmann and her many contemporaries, like Irma Grese, Elizabeth Volkenrath, etc would have been fully indoctrinated with the idea that all non-Aryan people were essentially worthless and represented a real danger to the German way of life and its racial purity. It is perhaps little wonder that so many of these former League members would eventually go on to become integral parts of the Nazi war machine, participating in some of the most vile and despicable actions against helpless civilians, who in their eyes were little more than vermin to be exterminated.

Once again, in common with a number of her more infamous contemporaries, Ruth Closius does not appear to have been an above average student and it has been suggested that having left school she simply drifted from one low paid job to another before deciding to settle down into married life. In July 1944 however, she was reported to have applied for work as a camp wardress and was initially sent to Ravensbruck concentration camp for training. Like Irma Grese, Ruth was said to have made an almost immediate impression with her superiors, treating the camp's female prison population with a level of cruelty that was much admired by the SS officials who administered the vast extermination centre.

Within a matter of weeks, Neudeck was thought to have been promoted to the rank of Block Overseer and was said to have been regarded by many of the prisoners, as one of the very worst female guards in the whole of Ravensbruck. A French inmate, testifying at the Ravensbruck War Crimes held by the British military authorities after the war, testified about one particular incident where Neudeck had used the sharp edge of a shovel to cut the throat of a prisoner who had somehow antagonised her.

In December 1944, Neudeck was transferred to the nearby extermination centre at Uckermark, which had formerly been used as a prison camp for young German girls who were deemed to be either criminal or difficult to manage. Now it was used to hold women from Ravensbruck, who were thought to be unfit for work or those that were over 52 years of age, but all of whom were destined to die in the gas chambers employed by the camp's Nazi commanders. Many of these women had been held in various concentration camps, often for years, sometimes for only a few months, but all had suffered both mentally and physically as a direct result of their harsh treatment and incarceration.

The fact that many were suffering from Typhus, Dysentery and starvation, their bodies wracked with disease, infected with lice and covered with festering cuts and wounds, seems to have mattered little to Ruth Neudeck and the other SS personnel stationed at Uckermark. Groups of selected prisoners would trudge to the camp daily, be forced to undress and stand naked for hours in all sorts of weather, while Neudeck, the infirmary nurse Vera Salvequart and the other guards would decide who was to live and who was to die. There is a suggestion that it was Neudeck herself, who carried a hooked cane that was used to catch hold of prisoners and drag them out of the ranks, before putting them to one side and assigning them to the barrack block which was used to hold those that were about to die. Most of the former prisoners who chose to testify at the post war Ravensbruck war crimes trials, remembered that these selections were more often than not just a purely arbitrary affair, with the SS guards simply choosing those that looked at them the wrong way or those who happened to stand out from the crowd for some reason.

During the time she was stationed at Uckermark, some 300 women a day were said to have perished in the mobile and static gas chambers which were employed there and was in addition to the hundreds of female inmates who inevitably died as a result of disease, starvation and lack of care. For the period from February 1945 to April 1945, a period covering some seven weeks, it was later reported by some independent sources that a total of some 7,000 women died in the Uckermark extermination centre.

Speaking prior to her trial in April 1948, Ruth Closius Neudeck fully admitted her complicity in the mistreatment and deaths of female prisoners held at both Ravensbruck and Uckermark and was said to have seemed proud of her actions and her achievements. In her statement to the military court, she boasted *"As I took over at Uckermark camp, there were around 4,000 prisoners of all nationalities there. When I was transferred some six weeks later, only 1,000 prisoners remained in the camp. During my time there around 3,000 women were selected for the gas chambers"*

She also testified to British military investigators *"When the vans were completely filled, the SS men and I drove to the crematorium where we unloaded the prisoners at a tool shed. In my role as Oberaufseherin I ordered them all to undress and when they had done so, a disguised SS man in a white coat brought the women, one by one, to another tool shed. When this shed was filled, it was then locked. Male prisoners were then ordered to enter the roof and I saw how they dropped something into an opening which was then closed. After the male prisoners had climbed down from the roof, the engines of the trucks were switched on, so that the screaming of the victims could not be heard."*

In March 1945, having completed her murderous task at Uckermark, Neudeck was thought to have been transferred to a sub-camp at Barth, a work camp associated with the production of Heinkel aircraft, where she continued her homicidal campaign against the resident prison population. However, in April 1945 the allied military forces drew closer to the camp and Neudeck along with her fellow SS guards were reported to have fled the prison and tried to disappear into the massing ranks of refugees and prisoners that were being driven towards the centre of Germany by the Soviet army. As with most of the defeated SS and regular German forces, Neudeck and her former camp comrades tried to make their way west, to where the British and American armies were based, rather than face the wrath of a Russian army who had seen millions of its citizens, killed, raped and imprisoned by the rapidly dissolving German forces and were keen to exact their own retribution on any individual who still wore the uniform of the hated SS or Gestapo.

Any hopes that Neudeck had, that she might somehow escape justice were short lived however. Along with a number of her former concentration camp colleagues she was subsequently arrested by British military forces and held while investigations were made into her involvement with the genocide that had taken place. In the meantime, although the Uckermark camp had been closed down in March 1945 following Neudeck's reign of terror, the sub-camp, along with the main centre at Ravensbruck were officially liberated by Russian forces on 30th April 1945, the men of the Red Army finally bringing an end to their years as places of human depravity and turning them instead into places of national disgrace.

As thousands of former concentration camp prisoners were finally released from their long captivities, so allied investigators began to receive the testimonies of those that had suffered at the hands of the individual SS female guards, including Ruth Closius-Neudeck. Hundreds of women from around Europe who had been imprisoned, starved, beaten and tortured at Ravensbruck bore witness to the cruelty of Neudeck, Binz, Grese, Volkenrath and the dozens of other Aufseherrin who had tried so hard to exterminate a whole generation of women that they considered to be both sub-human and worthless.

For the relatively small number of camp guards who were brought to trial after the war, their crimes were exacerbated by the fact that they had willingly participated in the torture and destruction of millions of people from the European continent, as well as a number of notable allied nationals, including the valiant SOE agents Violette Szabo, Denise Bloch, Cecily Lefort and Lilian Rolfe, all of whom bravely met their end in the misery that was Ravensbruck.

For Ruth Closius-Neudeck, there was little to say that could ever begin to defend her actions, or indeed her boastful acknowledgement of the fact that she had been primarily responsible for sending at least 3,000 innocent women to their deaths in the Uckermark camp's gas chambers. It came as little surprise then, to those watching the proceedings in April 1948, when the British Military Tribunal returned a guilty verdict on the 28-year-old former overseer and sentenced her to be hung, a death sentence which was carried out on the morning of the 29th July 1948 by Britain's official executioner Albert Pierrepoint.

22. THE ANONYMOUS MURDERER

IDA SCHREITER

Convicted of War Crimes at Ravensbruck concentration camp

Of the ten former female SS camp guards executed by the British military authorities following the end of World War II, Ida Schreiter is the one individual about whom, little if anything is known. Publicly available records suggest that she was born on the 27th December 1912 and served as an Aufseherin or wardress at the Ravensbruck concentration camp sometime between 1939 and 1945 and was subsequently executed by the British on 20th September 1948 at Hameln Prison by Albert Pierrepoint.

Clearly however, she was a war criminal of some note, given that she was given an equal sentence to that of the other nine female guards including the notorious Irma Grese, Elisabeth Volkenrath and Dorothea Binz, all of whom were infamous for their individual brutality and the cold indifference that they showed to the prisoners in their charge.

It seems fairly certain to assume therefore, that when Schreiter was finally brought to trial at the 7th Ravensbruck Trial, held between the 2nd and 21st July 1948 at Hamburg, that there was sufficient documentary evidence and witness testimonies to safely convict her of the charges laid against her. In the dock with her, was Emma Anna Maria Zimmer, the former Chief Overseer at Ravensbruck, who was said to have personally selected thousands of female prisoners for the camp's gas chambers and who ultimately, received a similar sentence from the court.

It is perhaps also worth noting for this particular guard, that various sources appear to have used entirely different names to identify her, including Gertrude Schreiter, Bertha Schreiter and Ida Schreider, all of which may have helped to distract reporters and confuse later records.

The principal charges laid against Schreiter, Zimmer, Luise Brunner, Anna Klein, Christine Holthower and Ilse Vettermann was that they had mistreated prisoners of allied nationalities and had participated in the selection of prisoners for the camps gas chambers. As with virtually all of the SS staff who were prosecuted by the various Allied Courts following the defeat of Nazi Germany, they were held to be equally culpable for the atrocities visited on any and all allied citizens or inmates who were imprisoned at their particular camp, generally being guilty by association as well as by individual deed. Consequently, most of the leading female guards at Ravensbruck were subsequently found to be responsible for the mistreatment and deaths of the many French, Polish, Russian and British women who were imprisoned in the "living hell" that the camp eventually became.

Some former guards tried to hide their identities and illicit actions and when accused by survivors simply claimed that the witness was mistaken or had a grudge against them. Others claimed that they were just following their superior's orders and accepted no personal responsibility for their actions whatsoever. Unfortunately for them however, the victorious Allies, who were still trying to come to terms with the very existence and the gross inhumanity of Germany's concentration camp system, were determined that someone should ultimately pay the price for the thousands of deaths, in which Ravensbruck and its staff had played a part. Its many female victims included Russian Red Cross nurses, the women of the French and Polish Resistance movements, Jewish women from throughout Europe, Jehovah's Witnesses, East European Gypsies, German Nationals who opposed the Nazi Party and of course the small, but vitally significant number of women who had lost their lives as members of Britain's Special Operations Executive, the SOE.

In common with their equally courageous sisters in mainland Europe, this relatively small number of British based women put aside their own lives and personal responsibilities, to play a part in helping to free Europe from the tyranny of Nazism. Selflessly, they put their very own existence at risk to help establish and maintain the national resistance movements that would go on to provide both vital intelligence and material support for the war effort, up to any beyond the Allied invasion of Europe on 6th June 1944 which led to the inevitable end of Hitler's declared 1000 year Reich. For a number of them, the gallantry that they displayed would sadly lead to their early deaths, as they were arrested, interrogated and tortured by the fearsome Gestapo, before finally being subjected to the rigorous and systemic brutality of the Nazi concentration camp at Ravensbruck.

Violette Szabo was born Violette Bushell on the 26th June 1921 in Paris to a French mother and an English father who worked as a driver in the city. Around 1935 however, the family were reported to have moved back to England, possibly as a result of the emergence of the Nazi Party in Germany, with the young Violette and her siblings finishing their education at the local school in Brixton.

At the outbreak of the second World War, she was thought to be working on the perfume counter of a London high street store when she met a young French Sergeant Major serving in the Foreign Legion called Etienne Szabo and for both it was clearly a case of love at first sight, as the pair were said to have married six weeks later, he was 31 and she was 19-years-old. Within a year or so the young couple were expecting their first child, but sadly Etienne was thought to have died from wounds he received at the Battle of El Alamein in October 1942 without ever having seen his new baby daughter Tania who Violette was now left to bring up alone.

She was already a member of Britain's Auxiliary Territorial Service and Etienne's death was thought to have provided the catalyst for Violette's later decision to volunteer for the SOE and help play a more active role in helping to defeat Nazi Germany. By April 1944 she was said to have completed the rigorous SOE training and was reputed to have become an accomplished markswoman, as well as being educated in unarmed combat, demolitions and wireless operations.

On the 5th April 1944 Violette undertook her first mission into occupied France, being dropped near Cherbourg to help re-establish a local resistance cell which had been decimated by the Germans. She was known to have actively participated in the sabotaging of vital infrastructure targets, as well as reporting on local factories that were producing materials for the German war effort and which could be attacked and put out of action by allied aircraft. Within a month she was recalled to England, her first tour as an SOE agent in the occupied territories deemed to be a resounding success.

Her second fateful mission was reported to have begun on 7th June 1944, D-Day plus one, as tens of thousands of allied troops, hundreds of military vehicles and unlimited munitions continued to pour ashore to support the long awaited liberation of Europe. Her immediate task was to help both interrupt and destroy German communication networks, thereby aiding the newly arrived allied troops to fully establish their military stronghold on the Normandy beaches.

Within days, Violette and her local resistance contacts were reported to be travelling in a car when they encountered a temporary roadblock and with the German troops being suspicious of the vehicle, a gun battle quickly ensued between the two parties. Rather than let the local resistance leader fall into enemy hands, Violette was said to have ordered him away from the scene while she held the advancing German troops at bay and was thought to have killed and wounded a number of the enemy before running out of ammunition and finally being overwhelmed by force of numbers.

She was subsequently handed over to the German Secret Police who were said to have interrogated her mercilessly, including beating and sexually assaulting her, in an effort to get Violette to disclose information on both her contacts and the local resistance networks. Refusing to submit or cooperate with the Nazi agents, she was then transferred to Fresnes Prison in Paris where she was held by the Gestapo, suffering further questioning, brutalities and privations, yet again refusing to provide them with any useful information. She was then transferred to Limoges Prison, where it was reported that the local resistance movement came within hours of launching a rescue mission for her, but were thwarted by the Germans, when they arranged for Violette to be sent to the women's concentration camp at Ravensbruck.

Incarcerated at Ravensbruck from August 1944, she was thought to have spent a few weeks there before being transported to the camp at Konigsberg in Eastern Prussia for a short period before being sent back to Ravensbruck once again. Quite why the German authorities chose to move Violette around is unclear, but the possibility exists that they feared she might be freed by the resistance, before they had a chance to execute her.

Sadly, the decision to execute Violette and her two SOE associates who were also being held in Ravensbruck at the same time was thought to have been made in February 1945. Early one morning, the three gallant agents were thought to have been taken out into an enclosed area between the camps barrack blocks and individually shot dead by SS Officers, who later arranged for the women's bodies to be destroyed in Ravensbruck's crematorium. She was 23-years-old when she died.

After the war, Britain posthumously awarded her the George Cross, the highest commendation that could be awarded, which was presented to her daughter Tania at Buckingham Palace by the king, George VI. The French government awarded her the Croix de Guerre and the Resistance Medal, as well as inscribing her name on the Roll of Honour at the SOE memorial in Valencay. Her wartime exploits and gallantry were later immortalised in the film "Carve her name with pride" and Odette Churchill a surviving SOE agent later described her as "the bravest of us all"

Cecily Lefort was born on 30th April 1900 as Cecily Mc Kensie and in 1924 was reported to have married a French doctor called Alex Lefort and settled down to a happily married life in France. At the outbreak of World War II however, Cecily and her husband relocated to England, at the same time allowing their home in France to be used by the resistance movement as a safe-house and meeting point.

As a fluent French speaker Cecily eventually volunteered for the French section of the Special Operations Executive, Britain's secret government agency that was charged with developing, training, arming and funding the many resistance and underground movements in mainland Europe, who were opposed to Hitler and his Nazi state.

Having received training as a wireless operator, as well being instructed in the use of unarmed combat, small weapons handling and general counter-intelligence techniques, in June 1943, Cecily along with two other SOE agents, Diane Rowden and Noor Inayat Khan, was flown into occupied France to begin their dangerous work.

In September 1943 Cecily was captured by the Nazi's and brutally interrogated by the Gestapo, before being taken to Fresne Prison in Paris where she was held in the most primitive of conditions, all the time being questioned and interrogated by members of the German security apparatus. Finally, after several months she was transferred to the female concentration camp at Ravensbruck where she was held and identified as a resistance worker. For the next 12 months she was reported to have endured the increasing levels of mistreatment, starvation and disease which was meted out to the whole of the camp's inmate population, as the Nazi penal system slowly but surely started to unravel.

By February 1945 the war was going badly for Hitler's German empire and throughout most of the concentration camps in mainland Europe, there was a rapid increase in activity as their commanders sought to eradicate the inmate populations, as well as evidence of the camps very existence. It was during this final phase of Ravensbruck's existence, that 45-year-old Cecily Lefort was thought to have finally succumbed to the privations, disease and mistreatment she had suffered during the months of her captivity, reportedly being sent to the gas chamber just three months before Ravensbruck was liberated by Russian forces.

Following the end of the war in Europe, Cecily Lefort was mentioned in dispatches for her services to Britain and as an active participant in the defence of France, the French government later awarded her the Croix de Guerre, as well as inscribing her name on the national SOE memorial which was raised at Valencay in France.

Denise Madeleine Bloch was a valiant young French woman who had more than one reason for her decision to take up arms and aid her country in resisting the military aggression of Nazi Germany. The daughter of a Jewish businessman from Paris, Denise was born in 1916 and during the years between the wars was brought up and educated in France, finally becoming a secretary for the Citroen car company sometime before the outbreak of World War II.

In 1942 she and her family were reported to have been arrested by the Gestapo in one of their regular purges, but were later thought to have been released by the Nazi investigators following their enquiries about the family. It was thought to be as a result of this experience that Denise became involved with the activities of the French Resistance movement, where she was said to have worked with the British SOE agent Brian Stonehouse.

By 1943 Denise was still active within the resistance movement and the decision was made to send her to Britain to receive training as an SOE operative, a journey which was thought to have involved her walking across the Pyrenees to reach the British naval base at Gibraltar, from where she was transported back to England.

By the following year, the 28-year-old had completed her training as an SOE wireless operator and in March of that year, just three months before the successful D-Day landings, was dropped back into occupied France to help establish a resistance unit in the Nantes region. Unfortunately, both she and her fellow SOE agent Robert Benoist were caught by the Gestapo and were ruthlessly interrogated and tortured in order to discover other members of their network. For her part, Denise was subsequently held at a number of locations, including Torgau and Konigsberg, before finally being sent to the female concentration camp at Ravensbruck.

Along with her SOE compatriot Lilian Rolfe, Denise was held for several months in the disease ridden camp, suffering the same mistreatment, starvation and slavery as the many other internees. Finally in around February 1945, as the German war machine began to collapse under mounting allied military pressure, the authorities at Ravensbruck began to impose the final Nazi edict of executing resistance fighters and enemy agents, reportedly shooting Denise and her fellow agents Violette Szabo and Lilian Rolfe, before destroying their bodies in the camp's crematoria.

After the war, Denise was posthumously awarded a Kings Commendation for Brave Conduct for her valiant actions against the enemy, by the British authorities. The French government also awarded her the Legion of Honour, the Croix de Guerre and the Resistance Medal, as well as inscribing her name on France's Roll of Honour at the SOE memorial at Valencay.

Lilian Rolfe was one of a pair of twin girls born to George Rolfe and his wife in Paris on 26th April 1914, the second baby girl being named Helen. The successful accountant's two young daughters spent much of their early lives being brought up and educated in France, as well as spending a significant amount of time visiting their paternal grandparents in England and travelling abroad with their parents. In around 1930 however, when Lilian and Helen were just sixteen the family were reported to have relocated to Brazil, where their father had found new employment and for the next few years the whole Rolfe family lived an idyllic lifestyle.

At the outbreak of World War II, the family were still well away from the conflict, although Lilian, now aged 25 was thought to be working as a secretary at the British Embassy in Rio de Janeiro. Possibly because her grandparents were still in Britain and seeing that the German war machine presented a real danger to both to her French homeland and her adopted England, Lilian was said to have returned to Britain to join the Women's Auxiliary Air Force and play her part in helping to defeat the Nazi menace.

As with other prospective SOE agents, it was Lilian's intimate knowledge of her French homeland and her obvious language skills which to first brought her to the attention of Britain's intelligence services who were already planning for the allied invasion of Hitler's European fortress. During 1943, the 29-year-old accountant's daughter underwent training as a wireless operator, as well as enduring the tough military training which was designed to help save her life as an undercover operative in the harsh environment of occupied France.

By April 1944 and having completed her training Lilian was then finally dropped back into her native homeland, with orders to help co-ordinate military resistance in the lead up to the allied invasion of Europe later that same year and where possible to disrupt German communication and supply lines. Although principally employed as a wireless operator, tasked to maintain communications between the various resistance groups and the allied headquarters in Britain, Lilian was reported to have actively participated in a number of military operations against German forces as well as their military assets and played a full part in helping to facilitate the successful Normandy landings which took place on the 6th June 1944.

Despite this invasion of Hitler's Europe by tens of thousands of allied troops, the situation for British agents and resistance fighters operating in the occupied territories remained perilous and the feared German Gestapo were reported to have substantially increased their efforts to hunt down and destroy these secret enemy cells. At Nargis in July 1944, Lilian and her comrades from the local resistance movement were finally cornered by the German forces, with the young SOE agent subsequently being captured and then transported to the infamous Fresne Prison in Paris, where she was said to have endured weeks of interrogation, torture and hardship, as the Gestapo tried to secure vital information from the fiercely resistant French woman.

Finally in August 1944, she was transferred to the concentration camp at Ravensbruck where, a German officer later reported to the allied authorities, Lilian was so ill because of her mistreatment that she could not walk unaided. For several months, the increasingly sick 30-year-old was thought to have been subjected to the same misery, starvation and disease ridden conditions that were inflicted on all of Ravensbruck's prisoner population as the German terror machine began to collapse under the strain of burgeoning prisoner numbers and diminishing resources, caused largely by allied advances into the occupied territories.

By the beginning of 1945 and with most German's recognising that the war was probably lost, the Nazi leadership, rather than capitulate, instead sought to increase the level of killing and genocide that they had been actively pursuing for the previous years. For captured resistance fighters and their allies particularly, their fate was almost guaranteed, as camp commanders sought to exact some sort of retribution for the inevitable destruction of Germany's armed forces and the allied dismantling of their beloved Third Reich.

Not content with having abused and mistreated the desperately ill Lilian Rolfe, who by now had been joined by the equally gallant Violette Szabo and Denise Bloch, the Ravensbruck authorities now decided to implement the highly illegal and completely unnecessary death sentences which had been passed on the three agents, along with hundreds of other women who had opposed the administration of Hitler and his Nazi party. Sometime in February 1945, the three women were reported to have been taken out to an open space between the camp's barrack blocks and simply shot down by the SS officers assigned that brutal task. It was only much later that allied investigators finally discovered that the bodies of the three murdered SOE operatives were later removed to the camp's crematoria, so that all evidence of their incarceration at Ravensbruck could be obliterated.

Following the end of the war in Europe, Lilian Rolfe was mentioned in Dispatches by the British and her name was engraved on the Runnymede memorial in Surrey. The French government awarded her the Croix de Guerre with Palm and her name was inscribed on the SOE "Roll of Honour" memorial at Valencay in France.

23. THE ALCOHOLIC AUFSEHERIN

EMMA ANNA MARIA ZIMMER

Convicted of War Crimes at Ravensbruck concentration camp

Born Emma Anna Maria Mezel at Schlutern in Germany on the 14th August 1888, she was yet another more mature German citizen who felt compelled to answer the Nazi party's call for volunteer's and at the same time set out to improve her own prospects and personal situation by choosing to work in one of Germany's emerging death camp's purely for better pay and conditions.

Reported to have begun her career as a camp guard at Ravensbruck in around 1939, Zimmer is thought to have been in one of the first intakes of German women who willingly volunteered to take on the role of "Aufseherin" or "Wardress" at the newly opened concentration camp. It was clearly a job that she was temperamentally well suited for, as she was reported to have progressed quickly to the rank of Chief Overseer at the camp, a title she was thought to have held from 1939 through to 1941.

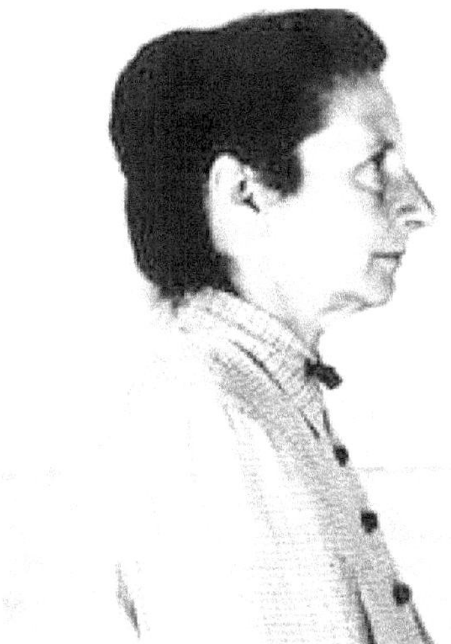

It was during this period that Zimmer was later accused of actively participating in the selection of specific prisoner's who were found to be suffering from mental illnesses or physical disorders, that were deemed to be incurable and which might well be inherited by future generations. To counter any possibility of such "tainted" blood entering the Nazi gene pool, the staffs at Ravensbruck, Buchenwald, Flossenburg and Sachsenhausen were reported to have actively sought out and identified prisoners who were suffering from either genetic or psychiatric afflictions and sent them to euthanasia centres like Bernberg, which was located near Magdeburg.

This mental hospital had been partially converted in 1940 to secretly dispose of Germany's sickest citizen's under the terms of a Nazi inspired euthanasia programme known as *Aktion T4* which was primarily designed to eradicate those German nationals who were deemed by nature of their illness, to be expendable, for the purpose of purifying the Aryan race. As with the later much larger death camps which were established throughout continental Europe, Bernberg was equipped with a gas chamber, that was designed to resemble a shower room and where the selected prisoners would ultimately die. The corpses were then transferred to another part of the buildings cellar complex, where two ovens had been installed, specifically for the purpose of disposing of the patients bodies.

In order to prevent any awkward questions being asked by the victims relatives, it was said to have been a common practice for the ashes of all the murdered patients to be dispensed into individual funeral urns, which were then returned to the grieving family's along with an official death certificate, stating that their loved on had succumbed to a generally common disease. Between 1941 and 1943 approximately 5,000 people were reported to have been liquidated at this one particular mental hospital, which was only one of the many established by the SS throughout Germany.

Most of the SS female camp guards who were recruited to staff the ever expanding numbers of Nazi concentration camps that were established from 1939 onwards were thought to be aged between 19 and 45 years of age, with those reaching the upper limit being transferred to other employment. For rare exceptions however, such as Emma Zimmer, exemptions seemed to have been made, allowing them to remain as "Aufseherrin" well beyond their 45th birthday. This was in part because of the dire shortage of suitable female candidates, the escalating numbers of prisoners being held and the natural viciousness of certain women who possessed the cold-blooded and dispassionate personalities needed to impose the Nazi will within these death camps.

Clearly Emma Zimmer displayed these much admired traits, as she was reported to still be employed at the highest level in Ravensbruck during the years 1939 to 1941, when she was said to be between 51 and 53 years of age. During these years she was also thought to have participated in the torture and ill-treatment of female prisoners who were confined within Ravensbruck's infamous "Bunker", the camp's prison compound where the much feared Dorothea Binz and Margaret Mewes, made their reputations for torturing and killing hundreds of female inmates.

Made up of a series of tiny prison cells, located on different levels, the "Bunker" was the punishment block for those women who infringed camp rules, for those that made an enemy of a particular camp guard or for specific high value prisoners, like the SOE agent Odette Sansom. For most ordinary inmates, who were sent there for physical punishment, their stay would typically involve them being starved, being deprived of all outside contacts, being mentally abused and physically tortured. The most common method of abusing these women was for them to be beaten with clubs and whips, having a vicious guard dog set on them or for their bodies to be misused in the most degenerative way. In almost all cases, these atrocities would only stop once the woman has passed out or had died from her torment.

From June 1943 through to January 1945 Zimmer remained at Ravensbruck, although it seems with a much lower level of responsibility, caused in part by her reportedly increasing reliance on alcohol to do her job properly. Along with other SS camp guards she was thought to have spent many hours drinking in the camp's canteen, no doubt discussing the many lethal events that had taken place, the parts that they had played and perhaps increasingly stiffening their own resolve to continue with the tasks that was being asked of them. Following the events of June 6th 1944 and the Allied landings at Normandy, along with the military reversals in the East, which saw the Red Army continuing to force the German forces back to their own national frontiers, it has also been reported that many of these same SS guards, were relying even more heavily on their alcohol rations simply to give them the courage to remain at their posts.

The rampant alcoholism that pervaded almost every SS run camp became such an issue for the SS leader, Heinrich Himmler, that it was rumoured he subsequently issued a national edict forbidding certain individuals from drinking any sort of alcoholic beverage, on pain of dismissal. It was possibly as a result of this particular order, that Emma Zimmer was reported to have been dismissed from her post at Ravensbruck in January 1945, her years of service and heavy drinking finally conspiring to make her both unreliable and unsuitable for the kind of work that would eventually be brought to an end some three months later. There is also some evidence that her general health was badly affected by both the disease and unsanitary conditions throughout the camp, with at least one source noting that she received treatment for a bout of Typhus, the lice borne illness which was endemic to most of the Nazi concentration camps.

Despite the fact that she had been dismissed prior to Ravensbruck being officially liberated by the Red Army on the 30th April 1945, Zimmer did not manage to avoid the inevitable accountability which was demanded by the victorious Allied armies. Arrested and held while investigations were made into her complicity with the Ravensbruck death camp, she was soon identified by a number of former inmates and indicted to stand trial for the mistreatment of Allied Nationals. Along with her former comrades, Gertrude (Ida) Schreiter, Luise Brunner, Anne Klein, Christine Holtower and Ilse Vettermann, Zimmer was arraigned before the British military court between 2nd and 21st July 1948. Of the six women who were tried Zimmer and Schreiter were found guilty of the main charges laid against them and were sentenced to be hung at Hameln Prison on 20th September 1948, the executions being carried out by Britain's official hangman, Albert Pierrepoint. Of the four remaining former camp guards, two were acquitted because of lack of evidence and the other two were given jail terms. Following their deaths on the scaffold, both Zimmer's and Schreiter's remains were interred in the prison's precincts.

24. A TRULY MURDEROUS MOOD

MARGARET "BILL" ALLEN

Convicted of murdering Mrs Nancy Chadwick

In a case that was perhaps reminiscent of the Susan Newell murder trial, the killing of 68-year-old Nancy Ellen Chadwick by 42-year-old Margaret "Bill" Allen appeared to be a random and motiveless act, perpetrated for no other reason than the accused woman having been in a "funny" mood. Unlike her Scottish counterpart however, Allen's actions have later been accounted for by some students of the case, because of her then unrecognised and undiagnosed psychological trans-gender issues, which they believe somehow played a part in the killing.

Reported to have been born in 1906, the third youngest of 22 children, Maggie Allen was said to have always been a bit of a "tom-boy", preferring to dress and act as a lad rather than the young girl that nature had deemed her to be. Throughout her formative years she was thought to have continued to adopt this more masculine persona, so by the time she had reached adulthood she was known and generally accepted as some sort of odd local character who preferred to be known as "Bill" rather than by her given names of Margaret or Maggie.

Both her working career and social life were said to have reflected her very masculine lifestyle, taking on jobs that typically might have been undertaken by men, such as a coalman and a bus conductor, a job from which she was eventually dismissed for being too physically rough with the passengers. In the local pubs and bars, rather than sit with the ladies in the much more comfortable lounge or snug, she would spend her evenings sitting in the often sparse public bars with the men, sharing their habits and their language, but no doubt still treated with a degree of suspicion by her fellow drinkers.

Her character was thought to have changed markedly in 1943 when her mother died, which might have accounted for her much more aggressive and less tolerant attitude, which would eventually get her fired from her job as a bus conductor. Her physical health was said to have suffered as a result of the deep and dark depressions that regularly beset her, as well as the heavy smoking and irregular diet she was noted for.

In the post war period and following her dismissal from the local bus company, Allen was said to have been employed in several of the local mills, as well as working as a post woman and finally been employed in a local slipper factor before losing that job for some unspecified reason. Clearly she was a hard worker and her regular employment posts were said to have allowed Allen to buy a property in the town on Bacup Road, one of the main routes in and out of Rawtenstall.

By August of 1948, Allen was said to have been between jobs and perhaps it was this situation, allied to depression over her personal life and a naturally aggressive attitude, that saw her temper primed to such a degree that even the most inconsequential act would cause her to react violently. So when a local 68-year-old woman called Mrs Nancy Chadwick called at Allen's home to borrow a cup of sugar, it seems that her unexpected and unwelcome visit provided the impetus for a sustained and murderous attack perpetrated by Margaret "Bill" Allen which would ultimately cost both women their lives.

Nancy Ellen Chadwick was the widow of a local wheelwright and well known in the town, who even at the age of 68 was still working as housekeeper for an 83-year-old local resident, as well as telling fortunes in the evenings which earned her a little more money. Despite her seemingly poor appearance, she was in fact a woman of means, having been left a number of properties in the town by a former employer from which she derived a regular weekly income. It was well known to many of the local residents that Mrs Chadwick would often sit on a bench in the local park counting her money, preferring to keep her money safe, because she didn't entirely trust banks. On at least one occasion however, this habit had rebounded on her, as she was robbed of her cash by a young man who had accosted her in the town centre, but still she failed to heed the warning.

Despite her regular income and the fact that she had money, it was reported that Nancy Chadwick was not simply careful with her money, but was mean; and would often try and cadge foodstuffs and the basics from her neighbours rather than pay for them herself. It was said to be because of this inherent meanness that she called at Maggie Allen's house late on a Saturday evening to borrow a cup of sugar and so incensed the irrational 42-year-old occupier that she lost her life as a consequence.

Allen would later tell the detectives who were investigating Mrs Chadwick's murder that the old woman just happened to catch her in one of her "funny" moods and had insisted on coming into her house. Margaret had just happened to look around the kitchen and saw the coal hammer lying there and on the spur of the moment simply picked it up and struck Nancy, causing her to yell out. The woman's shout seemed to incite Allen even more and she struck her many more times, but could not tell the officers exactly how many times.

With her elderly neighbour lying dead on the floor, Allen then made her second mistake, by searching through the old woman's clothing and belongings for any money or personal items that she wanted to take. As she rummaged through Mrs Chadwick's clothing she discovered a secret pocket in her under skirt where money and valuables could be secreted and quickly removed what was there. With the body now stripped of Nancy's hidden treasures, it only remained for Allen to dispose of the corpse itself and this was where she made her third mistake.

Possibly in the late hours of Saturday 28th August 1948 or the early hours of the next day, Sunday the 29th August, Maggie Allen seems to have devised a plan which would allow Nancy Chadwick's body to be discovered, with the woman appearing to have been killed as the result of a road accident. With her own in-depth knowledge of the local bus network and having lived by the main route in and out of the town for an extended period of time, Allen was thought to have carried or dragged the lifeless body into the roadway and placed it in such a way as to mimic hit-and-run accident, whilst at the same time hoping that the corpse might be hit by a passing vehicle, which would further obscure the injuries that she herself had caused.

At the same time the inept murderess was thought to have disposed of her victim's handbag in the waters of the nearby River Irwell, but instead of discarding the murder weapon in a like fashion was said to have continued using the coal hammer, which would ultimately help detectives prove her involvement in the crime. She also failed to make sure that the crime scene itself had been sufficiently cleaned to avoid any detection by the Police officers who would almost inevitably turn up at her door.

Pretty quickly her ill thought out plans began to go awry. Unfortunately for Allen, Nancy Chadwick's body remained untouched on the main thoroughfare and when a bus carrying union members back from a meeting in the early hours of the Sunday morning did come along, the driver was aware enough of the bundle, lying in the road that he managed to stop the vehicle, without having run over it. Upon inspection, the driver recognised that the bundle was in fact the body of an elderly woman and quickly despatched someone to contact the local Police. Within a short time two uniformed officers were reported to be on the scene, taking statements from the driver and passengers and roping the area off to protect the now covered body from prying eyes.

By eight o'clock that Sunday morning, Mrs Chadwick's body had been taken to the local morgue for an autopsy to be carried out, which soon revealed that the woman had not been the victim of a hit-and-run accident, but had been deliberately murdered. Perhaps because there had never been a single recorded instance of a murder in the Rawtenstall area, the Police investigation was handed over to Chief Superintendent Woodmansey of Lancashire C. I. D., who almost immediately requested help from Scotland Yard, who provided aid in the form of Detective Chief Inspector Steven's and Detective Sergeant Thompson, two highly experienced officers.

Following the preliminary post mortem performed by Dr Gilbert Bailey and the formal identification which was carried out by Mrs Chadwick's nephew William Barnes, officers began searching for the dead woman's handbag that was known to be missing. Using Nancy's hat and coat as a scent source, the Police were reported to have brought in a bloodhound called "Lubit" who very quickly traced the bag to the banks of the river where it had been thrown into the shallows. As officers in waders walked through the water looking for the dead woman's discarded belongings their attention was said to have been drawn to a particular spot by a member of the watching crowd, who later turned out to be a local resident, Margaret "Bill" Allen.

Although not unknown in some murder cases, where the murderer actively involves themselves in the subsequent Police investigation, the fact that Allen deliberately put herself at the forefront of public interest in the crime was eventually noticed. Locals would also later testify in court that "Bill" Allen seemed to know a lot about the dead woman, of her regularly counting her money in the park and the fact that she had a secret pocket in her underskirt, a fact which would only have been known to Nancy Chadwick's most intimate friends, or indeed to her murderer.

Finally, forensic evidence found at the scene pointed detectives in the right direction and on the Wednesday following the discovery of Nancy Chadwick's body; officers were knocking on the front door of the house owned by Margaret Allen. Almost straight away they noticed bloodstains on the walls of the house, just inside of the doorway, with later searches uncovering blood evidence in the coal cellar of Allen's home, carried there by the bloodied hammer which she had failed to dispose of following the murder. Police were also thought to have recovered a number of items from the house which clearly belonged to the old woman and could only have been taken after she had died.

Arrested on suspicion of murdering her 68-year-old neighbour, Allen was taken to Rawtenstall Police Station where she was subsequently questioned by the murder squads leading officers and by the afternoon of the same day was said to have admitted her crime. She was reported to have been fairly compliant and calm when she was formally charged with capital murder and even thanked the officers as she was led to the cells. The following day Allen was arraigned at the local court and was thought to have been remanded to the custody of Manchester Strangeway's Prison until her trial, which began on the 8th December 1948.

Brought to trial at Manchester Assizes on that date, the whole case was reported to have lasted some five hours, with the jury returning a guilty verdict within 15 minutes of being asked to consider the evidence. Unsurprisingly, the judge imposed a death sentence on the female prisoner who stood in the dock before him, but who quite naturally dressed herself as a man.

Following the imposition of the capital sentence, which was due to take place on the 12th January 1949, there was thought to be a limited but unsuccessful campaign to have the sentence commuted to a life term, which even Margaret Allen believed would be successful. Unfortunately for her, there appeared to be little appetite amongst either politicians or the general public to have her death warrant repealed and even in her hometown of Rawtenstall only a couple of hundred people out of a local population of some 30,000 felt compelled to sign a petition organised by a friend of Allen's, a Mrs Annie Cook.

When the appeal was officially denied by the Home Secretary, Allen was reported to have been both surprised and angered by the governments decision and was said to have spent the final days of her life in a highly belligerent and argumentative mood, never expressing any remorse for taking the life of her neighbour Nancy Chadwick.

At eight o'clock on the morning of 12th January 1949 Albert Pierrepoint, the official executioner stepped into the condemned cell at Manchester Strangeway's Prison to administer the punishment imposed by the courts and bringing an end to Margaret "Bill" Allen's turbulent and troubled life. The prison chaplain would later proclaim to the press that she had met her end in a manner befitting a man and that Margaret Allen had in fact behaved in a much braver way than some men he had witnessed. It was also said to be his honest opinion that no woman should ever be hung and that he considered it to be morally wrong that the country should continue to do so.

Regardless of the Reverend's personal opinion on Capital Punishment and its imposition on convicted female murderers, it is entirely clear that Margaret Allen deliberately and wilfully killed her neighbour Mrs Nancy Chadwick in a fit of unrestrained anger, over which the victim had little if any control. Any suggestion that Allen's trans-gender issues should or could have been used as mitigation for her actions on that fateful Saturday night should not and ultimately were not regarded as reasonable or justifiable and as a consequence she was found to be culpable.

Bearing in mind that she was able to provide detectives with a fairly clear and rational explanation of the night's events, as well as her own feelings and more importantly her state of mind, it was clear to the court that she was not insane at the time that she committed the murder. Her subsequent actions, of robbing the corpse of its valuables, devising a way to dispose of the body, by trying to make the death look like a hit-and-run incident and throwing away the victim's belongings, all suggested a degree of thought and planning on her part and were not seen as being indicative of someone who was suffering from any sort of mental aberration.

Her previously recorded character and unruly masculine type behaviour, especially her physically assaulting and bullying passengers while she was employed as a bus conductor undoubtedly helped to convince the jury that Margaret Allen was purely and simply a highly aggressive individual who was unwilling or unable to control her violent temper. It was that particular facet of her personality which allowed her to commit murder and it was that which ultimately condemned her in the jury's eyes, although her appearance in the dock, dressed in rather unconventional masculine attire would not have helped the men and women of the jury relate to the prisoner that stood before them.

25. A SPOONFUL OF JAM AND RODINE

LOUISA MAY MERRIFIELD

Convicted of murdering her employer Mrs Sarah Ricketts

When 79-year-old bed-ridden Sarah Ricketts advertised for a couple to act as her live-in housekeeper and handyman, she was thought to have been inundated with applications from married couples who were anxious to secure a position in the famous northern beach resort of Blackpool. Unfortunately for her however, it appears that most of the couples that applied for the post were either unsuitable or were quickly put off accepting the position by the behaviour and habits of the old lady herself.

Despite her apparent wealth and respectability, suggested by both her comfortably modern bungalow and her ability to employ live-in staff, Sarah was thought to be a no-nonsense, plain speaking working class woman who had the money to indulge a fairly peculiar lifestyle and dietary regime. It was said that the nearly 80-year-old woman would commonly eat a meal of glycerine and jam, washed down with a tot of rum and a bottle of stout, delivered to her room by the resident staff.

Reported to be a highly irritable and demanding employer, the person who immediately appealed to Mrs Ricketts was 46-year-old Louisa May Merrifield, who along with her husband, 71-year-old Alfred Merrifield seemed to be just the sort of people she was looking for, caring, considerate and perhaps more importantly, a couple that appeared to be compliant.

Sadly though, the old lady had obviously and totally misjudged the couple and that proved to be a critical mistake which would ultimately cost her life. In reality, Louisa Merrifield was a convicted fraudster who had an equally poor temperament as the old lady herself and was reported to have had more than 20-odd jobs in the previous three year period, none of which she could sustain. Her private life was said to have been as chaotic as her working career, having been married three times and with her two children being taken into care, ostensibly as a result of her heavy drinking and unreasonable behaviour.

Her third husband, Alfred Merrifield, was thought to be the perfect partner for the overtly dominant Louisa, a simple compliant individual who would later be reported as an innocent partner in the murderous machinations of his wife, but whose actions to this day remain highly questionable.

Although Louisa and Albert were thought to have undertaken their duties in an exemplary fashion for the first few days, within two weeks of having been employed by Sarah Ricketts, the old lady's doctor was surprised by the new housekeepers request that he certify his patient sane enough to make a new will. Despite any doubts or suspicions he may have had however, it seemed clear that Mrs Ricketts was so taken by her new employees that she had decided to change her will, leaving her home and possessions to the kindly Mr and Mrs Merrifield; so in spite of any personal misgivings the doctor felt compelled to provide the necessary confirmation.

However, when the old lady suddenly died within weeks of signing the new will and for no obviously apparent reason, then the lingering doubts held by the medic once again resurfaced. As in the case of Ethel Major, these concerns were further added to by Louisa Merrifield's request that Mrs Ricketts remains should be cremated and that she had not wanted her family notified of her death. As before, the local authorities were quick to authorise an autopsy on the dead woman's body, subsequently finding that the cause of death was due to phosphorus poisoning, which was commonly associated with the rat poison Rodine.

As soon as the cause of death was confirmed, the Police were informed and an investigation begun into the suspicious death of Sarah Ricketts. As the poison Rodine could only be sourced from local chemists, detectives quickly began canvassing local pharmacists and quickly identified the shop where Alfred Merrifield had recently purchased a container of the rat killing agent. However, when they searched Mrs Ricketts former home, now legally occupied by the Merrifield's, they found no evidence of the poison remaining in the property.

Despite this, the official investigation continued and it wasn't long before the Police started receiving information from acquaintances of Louisa Merrifield who told them that the former housekeeper had previously bragged about a property inheritance that she had been left by an old lady. When these friends had pressed her on the matter, Louisa had admitted that in fact the old lady wasn't dead yet, but soon would be. With what almost amounted to a full confession, the Police immediately arrested and charged Louisa and Alfred Merrifield on suspicion of murdering their former employer, Sarah Ricketts.

The husband and wife were jointly brought to trial on the 20th July 1953 at Manchester Assizes, with the prosecution laying out their largely circumstantial case before the jury. The Crown alleged that the couple, having ingratiated themselves with the old lady to the point that she had changed her will in their favour, then systematically poisoned her until she succumbed to the inevitable result of ingesting such a product. The prosecution speculated that the Rodine, rather than being used for its true purpose, had in fact been added to Mrs Ricketts favourite blackcurrant jam which she ate straight from the jar, by the spoonful.

The court testimony of Louisa's former acquaintances, who she had told of the expected inheritance further strengthened the Crown's case against her and underlined the idea of the woman referred to being Sarah Ricketts and not some other imaginary benefactor.

As with the earlier cases of Edith Thompson, Charlotte Bryant and Emily Swann, Louisa's personal life became as much a feature of her trial as did any substantive evidence put before the court. The fact that she was seen as an indolent and aggressive alcoholic, who had virtually abandoned two husbands and her two children, was guaranteed to paint her in the worst possible light from the jury's perspective, which could quite easily see such a woman calmly and calculatingly poisoning a frail and bed-ridden invalid who had something that she wanted.

It was also reported that Louisa had tried to defend herself in court by attacking the character of the dead woman, who clearly could no longer defend her own reputation. The allegations made by the accused woman were to said to be of such a nature that the trial judge publicly described them as being "vulgar", suggesting that Louisa was attempting to undermine both Sarah Ricketts reputation and her femininity. As it turned out, this defensive strategy proved to be catastrophic to her case, as it simply destroyed any sympathy the juror's might have felt for her and reinforced the prosecutions view that she was a deliberately wicked individual who would use any ruse to justify her criminal acts.

Her alleged accomplice, Alfred, seems to have been treated and seen in an entirely different light, much of which was undoubtedly due to his age and an implicit acceptance that he was a simpleton, who had been adversely affected by his domineering wife, Louisa. Despite the fact that it was Alfred who had purchased the Rodine from the local pharmacy and was said to have deliberately hindered those that were involved in the murder investigation, much of this appears to have been dismissed purely as the actions of a rather geriatric old man, whose trust had been abused by a cunning spouse.

At the end of the murder trial, it came as little surprise to many observers that Louisa May Merrifield was found guilty of killing her former employer Sarah Ricketts. However, it did come as a surprise to some, that the jury were undecided as to the guilt her co-accused Alfred Merrifield and as a result he was discharged by the court, later inheriting half of the estate of his former employer.

Sentenced to hang at eight o'clock in the morning at Manchester Strangeway's Prison on Friday 18th September 1953, there was a campaign to have Louisa Merrifield's death sentence commuted to a life sentence, which might have seen her serve a 12 year jail term. However, the government of the day were thought to be determined to adhere to the general rule that those that killed with poison were never reprieved and so all appeals on behalf the Blackpool housekeeper were refused.

She was to see Alfred one last time, in the condemned cell of her prison, just days before her death. As they parted for the final time, she was reported to have said "Goodbye Alfie. Look after yourself and God Bless". On the morning of the 18th July she was hanged on the gallows by Britain's principal executioner Albert Pierrepoint, with her later autopsy proving that she died instantly. Louisa's body was later interred within the precincts of Manchester Strangeway's, close to those of Margaret Allen and Louie Calvert.

26. THE MURDEROUS MOTHER-IN-LAW

STYLLOU CHRISTOFI

Convicted of murdering her daughter-in-law Hella Christofi nee Bleicher

Born on the British dependency of Cyprus in 1900, Styllou Pantopiou Christofi was reported to be a member of the islands largely Greek community, who along with most of her contemporaries was brought up with no formal education, which left her almost illiterate and with little opportunity to venture outside of her own small village, the foundations of which were firmly built on a family's traditions and its heritage.

Perhaps because of the intense insularity that such isolated villages generated within themselves, personal disagreements and arguments within the community, were often seen as a matter for those that lived there, perhaps leading to levels of behaviour or resolutions that the wider world might consider improper or unreasonable, but which to the village itself were seen as entirely acceptable.

In 1925, Styllou Christofi was reported to have been charged with killing her mother-in-law by forcing a burning torch down the older woman's throat, purely as a result of the two women not being able to get along with one another. This crime, had it taken place in most modern countries of the period, would almost certainly have resulted in her receiving a lengthy jail term if not the death penalty, but this was not the case in Cyprus. Rather, the court was reported to have taken the view that Styllou had been so seriously provoked by her mother-in-law, that her actions, although extreme, were not sufficiently serious enough to warrant a prison term.

Regardless of the reasons for her escaping any sort of judicial punishment for her murderous actions, the event was undoubtedly pivotal, in that Styllou was subsequently released to commit her second known killing some 20-odd-years later that would bring her to the attention of the British public.

Although little is known of her life following the death of her mother-in-law, it was entirely likely that Christofi simply returned to her village life, becoming a familiar face within her own small community and raising a family. Her only known son, Stavros, was reported to have left Cyprus sometime during the 1940's, eventually making his way to London, finding himself a job as a wine waiter and settling down with his wife, a German born shop assistant called Hella Bleicher, with whom he had three children.

In 1953 and not having seen her son for over 12 years, Styllou Christofi was reported to have made the journey to England to see Stavros, his new wife and more importantly her three grand-children, who she had never seen before. On arriving at her son's Hampstead home, it soon became clear to the Greek matriarch that her grand-children were being raised to be typically English children, who had little interest in or knowledge of their Greek heritage or language. For a woman who had been brought up on and fully embraced the native culture and history of Greece this was an entirely unacceptable situation which she was bound and determined to rectify regardless of any objections.

Matters were made increasingly worse by the fact that she and her new daughter-in-law were unable to communicate easily with one another and that both women had entirely different ideas of how the children should be raised. Almost inevitably Stavros found himself constantly having to arbitrate between the two women and it soon became clear to all three parties that the current situation could not be allowed to continue and that something needed to be done to resolve the festering problem.

Finally, in the July of 1953 Stavros and his wife agreed that Hella should take the three children on a trip to Germany, during which time he would try and persuade his mother to return home to Cyprus. Unfortunately for the couple, Styllou obviously became aware of the plan and seems to have made up her mind that Hella was responsible for the problems between them and that with her out of the way, she would be able to stay in England and help raise her grand-children in a more traditional way.

On the evening of 29th July 1953, with Stavros having left for work and the three children safely tucked up in bed, Styllou put her quickly conceived and ill-thought out plan into action. While Hella was distracted with her chores, her mother-in-law struck her on the head with a heavy ash tray from the boiler, knocking her bloodied and unconscious to the floor of the family kitchen. Styllou then took hold of a scarf which was lying nearby and proceeded to strangle the subdued Hella until she was dead.

With the lifeless body now at her disposal, the hapless mother-in-law then set about using paper and paraffin, to set fire to the corpse. A neighbour called Young, who happened to be out with his dog, noticed the glow of the fire and seeing what he thought was a mannequin being burnt inside the house was about to investigate further when he noticed Styllou Christofi attending to the blaze and so passed by instead.

How Christofi had hoped to explain Hella's mysterious death is unclear, but it has been suggested that she hoped to convince people that her daughter-in-law had either died as the result of an accident or had unexpectedly committed suicide. Either way it did not matter, as the blaze which she had started to dispose of the body was thought to have quickly gotten out of control and within minutes began to threaten the entire house, with her grand-children still asleep inside.

In a state of panic, Styllou was said to have run out into the street seeking help from passers-by, finally finding a couple called Burstoff who were parked up outside of the local railway station. In broken English she explained that there was a fire in the house and that children were asleep inside and beckoned for the couple to come and help her rescue them.

Rushing to the scene to evacuate the children, the couple obviously had the presence of mind to call the fire brigade and with everyone safely out of the building were more able to fully take in the scene that presented itself to them. The source of the fire soon became self evident and having identified the partially burnt corpse lying in the kitchen, the Police were summoned to investigate the strange events at the Hampstead property; and it wasn't long before the neighbouring dog-walker had contacted the investigators to tell them what he had seen earlier in the evening.

Hella's burnt body clearly showed the signs of strangulation and the hastily cleaned bloodstains on the kitchen floor clearly indicated that an attack had occurred there first, with the dead woman having been first beaten and strangled later on. A detailed examination and search of both the body and property revealed that Hella Christofi's wedding ring had been removed prior to the fire, later turning up in Styllou Christofi's bedroom, for which the mother-in-law could offer no reasonable explanation.

Arresting the 53-year-old Greek grand-mother on suspicion of murdering her daughter-in-law Hella, Police soon arranged for an interpreter to attend Styllou's formal interview, during which she was asked to offer an explanation for the evening's events. Still denying any wrongdoing, the prisoner told detectives that she had come downstairs to the kitchen and found Hella lying on the floor already alight. She had tried to put the flames out with water and had attempted to wake her daughter-in-law by touching her face, but Hella had not moved, so she thought that she must be dead.

Clearly her version of events did not match with the evidence found by the Police and they had already eliminated the possibility of a stranger having committed the murder, so it became obvious that there was only one possible suspect, Styllou Christofi. She was subsequently charged with the murder of her daughter-in-law and remanded into custody at Holloway Prison.

Styllou was brought to trial at the Old Bailey on 28th October 1954 and the prosecution case against her was so overwhelming that her defence counsel advised his client to plead insanity, but she refused and was consequently found guilty of capital murder. Sentenced to death by the trial judge, there was a limited campaign to have her sentence commuted, but given the nature of the crime and the emerging details of her earlier murder in Cyprus, the British media were not thought to be inclined to support a widespread appeal against her punishment.

Although there undoubtedly were grounds for an appeal, given her mental state and her earlier history of violent outbursts, including the murder of her mother-in-law in Cyprus, it seems clear that the government of the day were not easily inclined to allow any plea for clemency. Consequently, her death sentence was confirmed for eight o'clock in the morning on 13th December 1954, the execution being assigned to Britain's principal hangman, Albert Pierrepoint.

Whilst being held in the condemned cell the violently jealous grand-mother was reported to have asked for a Maltese cross to be hung in the room to help her with her religious devotions. The request was granted by the prison authorities and the icon was thought to have remained in place until 1967 when the room was finally dismantled, following Britain's abolition of the death penalty.

Following Christofi's execution and her subsequent autopsy which determined that her death was instantaneous, her body was buried in an unmarked grave within the prison's precincts. However, in around 1971 and during a rebuilding programme undertaken at the prison the bodies of Styllou, Edith Thompson, Amelia Sachs and Annie Walters were exhumed and later re-interred in a single plot at Brooklands Cemetery in Surrey.

27. THE INTENTIONAL KILLER

RUTH ELLIS

Convicted of murdering her lover, racing car driver David Blakely

For older generations of the British public, the execution of Ruth Ellis remains a pivotal moment in the long fought campaign to finally remove Capital Punishment from the statute books, even though the perpetrator herself clearly accepted the concept and practice of judicial retribution and according to some reporters even willingly welcomed the very idea of paying for her crime with her own life.

Born on the 9th October 1926 in the North Wales seaside resort of Rhyl, Ruth Hornby was one of five children born to Arthur Neilson a professional musician and his wife Bertha, a Belgium national who had settled in Britain. Although the family's original surname was said to be Hornby, Arthur seems to have adopted the name Neilson, either as a professional stage name or for some other unknown reason, but by the time the family had relocated to London in around 1941; Neilson was their generally accepted surname.

The young Ruth was thought to have left school at 14 years old and found work in a number of low paid and often unskilled jobs, such as a waitress or shop worker, rather than finding employment in any of the extensive war-time industries which were always looking to recruit new workers. Perhaps these casual positions offered her the opportunity to exploit and be a part of the vibrant social scene which existed in London at that time, the city being populated by cash rich servicemen from across the Atlantic who were keen to have a good time in the capital.

In 1944, at the age of 17, Ruth was reported to have become pregnant by a Canadian serviceman, who was said to have kept in touch with her and helped her financially only until he returned home after the war. Now left alone with her baby boy Andre to take of, Ruth was thought to have entered the seedy world of Britain's post war nightclub scene where she managed to find work as a hostess, a role which had obvious associations with both the criminal fraternity and female prostitution.

Six years later, in 1950, she was known to have married George Ellis, a 41-year-old divorced dentist who was a customer at the club where Ruth worked. Said to have been a chronic drinker who became extremely aggressive after taking alcohol, Ellis' often unreasonable behaviour was well matched by Ruth's own possessive and jealous nature, which inevitably resulted in the marriage failing within a very short period of time. From the relationship however, Ruth had a baby girl called Georgina who was born in 1951, but because of the marital breakdown Ellis was said to have refused to publicly acknowledge the little girl as being his legitimate child.

Now with two small children to take care of and financially maintain, Ruth was said to have moved back to her parent's home for a period, before resuming her career as a nightclub hostess. It was through this work that she was thought to have met a number of minor celebrities, including Diana Dors, the British film and television actress who was said to have helped Ruth obtain a "bit" part in the film "Lady Godiva Rides Again", although her role was a minor one and not credited.

By 1953, Ruth was the manageress of a small private nightclub called the "Little Club" and it was here that she was thought to have first met the man who would have such a fateful impact on her life. David Blakely was a former public schoolboy, who was a motor engineer turned racing car driver and an individual with highly expensive tastes. Although three years younger than her and from a totally different social background, Blakely and Ruth were reported to have soon become involved with one another and within weeks they were said to be sharing her living accommodations above the club.

The relationship soon blossomed into something far more serious than a casual love affair and it was even reported that Blakely had proposed marriage to Ruth, despite the fact that he was already said to be engaged to another woman. Perhaps desperate to find true happiness, Ruth was thought to have accepted his proposal, even though she was still legally married to the alcoholic George Ellis who had subsequently abandoned Ruth and her two small children.

Unfortunately for her, her acceptance of Blakely's proposal then began to cause problems for the pair, as her fiancés increasing jealousy of Ruth's male customers began to cause divisions and arguments between the two of them. Perhaps believing that Ruth might be unfaithful to him, Blakely was said to have spent an increasing amount of time at the club, aggressively warning off any male customers that might try to flirt with the extremely attractive hostess and as a consequence the business began to suffer, as did Ruth's own earnings.

With their relationship increasingly fraught and fuelled by excessive drinking, both Ruth's and Blakely's personal lives were further complicated by their individual involvement with third parties. For her part, Ruth was thought to have had a friendship with a customer called Desmond Cussens, which may or may not have been intimate, but all the same Cussens was said to have disliked Blakely with a passion. At the same time that he was engaged to Ruth, David Blakely was said to be conducting an affair with another unnamed woman, but whether Ruth was aware of this relationship or not is unclear.

By March 1955 and despite their faltering relationship, Ruth was reported to be pregnant by Blakely and possibly hoped that finally things would begin to improve between them. Unhappily for both of them, during one of their many frequent and violent quarrels, Blakely was said to have struck Ruth in the stomach causing her to miscarry their unborn child, although she was later said to have denied that the blow was deliberate or had caused her to lose the baby.

Despite the physical and emotional trauma of losing their unborn child, Ruth forced herself to go and watch Blakely race his car, the Emperor, on the 1st April 1955, but unfortunately for him the engine was reported to have blown up prior to the race and rather typically he seems to have blamed Ruth for the mishap. Perhaps because of her already physically weakened state and the emotional strain of being blamed for something that was clearly not her fault, Ruth was said to have been extremely ill for a few days, during which Blakely was said to be both devoted and caring towards her.

As her health slowly improved, the couple were said to have planned to spend the forthcoming Easter weekend together and according to their friends all seemed well between them. However, on the morning of Friday 8th April 1955, Blakely was reported to have gone out, having told Ruth that he would return later in the day to take her out for a drink with some mutual friends, the Findlaters, but he never came back. Perhaps irritated by his unexplained absence Ruth was later said to have gone to the Findlater's flat and demanded that Blakely come out and talk to her, but he refused and it was only when the Police were called that she finally left the area.

Over the next day or so Ruth was said to have become increasingly obsessed about Blakely's whereabouts and the reasons for his continuing refusal to talk with her and would later tell people that by the Sunday evening she had finally developed the peculiar idea of killing her erstwhile lover. She would also later tell detectives that she had spent much of the weekend drinking with an unnamed male friend, who many believe was Desmond Cussens and had told him that if she had a gun she would kill Blakely. Unfortunately for Ruth, her companion then informed her that he did indeed have access to a gun and later took her to Epping Forest to show her how to use it, before driving her to Hampstead and her fateful meeting with David Blakely.

On the Sunday evening of the Easter weekend, Ruth and her companion had spotted Blakely drinking at the Magdala public house, but rather than confront him in the tavern itself, she was reported to have waited outside until he returned to his car. At around 9.20 pm Blakely came out of the Magdala and Ruth attracted his attention by calling over to him, but he was said to have ignored her hails and continued on towards his car. Pulling the .38 calibre revolver from her handbag, Ruth walked across the street towards her lover and levelling the gun at him, pulled the trigger for the first time. Although this first shot was thought to have missed its target, the sound of its discharge was thought to have been enough to cause the startled Blakely to duck down behind his car, but not before he had been struck by a second round fired by Ruth who was now advancing towards him. As he lay wounded on the pavement, she was said to have quickly rounded the vehicle and stood over him before firing the remaining four bullets into his prone body, one of which was fired from such a close range that it actually burned Blakely's skin. It would later transpire that at least one of the guns rounds had ricocheted off the pavement and struck an innocent passer-by Mrs Gladys Yule in the hand, an event which was later used as a contributory factor in the British Governments absolute refusal to commute Ruth Ellis' death sentence.

Having fatally wounded David Blakely, Ruth apparently made no effort to escape the scene, but simply stood clutching the murder weapon in her hand, until it was taken off her. Customers from the Magdala and passers-by who had heard the gunshots inevitably came to investigate the commotion, including an off-duty policeman called Alan Thompson, who was said to have disarmed Ruth and held her until his uniformed colleagues arrived at the scene. Arrested on suspicion of murder, she was then taken to Hampstead Police Station and questioned by detectives who later reported Ruth to be calm and collected and not under the influence of either drink or drugs, although it was later suggested that she had taken copious amounts of both over that fateful weekend. She was said to have made a full and frank confession to the investigators and was subsequently charged with the wilful murder of

David Blakely and was held until the following day, Easter Monday, where she was arraigned at a special sitting of Hampstead Magistrates Court.

Remanded into custody at Holloway Prison, Ruth was initially held in the prison's hospital wing and was interviewed by Holloway's chief medical officer, Mr M R Williams who later reported that he had found no evidence of mental illness in the prisoner. In preparation for the later murder trial, she was also said to have been examined by two different psychiatrists, one for the defence and one for the prosecution, neither of whom found her to be suffering from any mental incapacity or impairment. Her old friend Desmond Cussens was thought to have instructed a solicitor called John Bickford to act for her during her subsequent arraignments and Cussens himself was reported to have visited Ruth every day at Holloway, up until the time of her trial.

The murder trial began on 20th July 1955 at the Old Bailey's No: 1 Court and was heard before Mr Justice Havers, with the prosecution team being led by Mr Christmas Humphrey's and the defence by Mr Aubrey Stevenson. Despite the advice of her legal team that she should try and appear demure and possibly tragic for the court, Ruth was reported to have appeared in the dock wearing a highly fashionable black two-piece suit, with a white blouse and her hair recently bleached platinum blonde. Although she knew that this look would possibly alienate her from some of the jurors who would ultimately decide her fate and her plea of "not guilty" was surprising to many reporters, it has been suggested by a number of those involved with the case that Ruth was not only being true to herself, but only ever wanted her day in court and was seemingly quite content with the idea that she would be found guilty of the crime and would subsequently hang for her actions.

Any hopes that her defence team had, that they might persuade the jury to return a verdict of guilty of manslaughter rather than murder were completely dashed when Ruth went into the witness box to be questioned by the prosecutor Mr Christmas Humphrey's. He asked her "When you fired the revolver at close range into the body of David Blakely, what did you intend to do"? to which Ruth replied "It's obvious when I shot him that I intended to kill him".

As soon as she had uttered these words, any hopes that her legal team might have had, that they could persuade the judge and jury that she had committed the crime while her mind was temporarily unbalanced, completely disappeared. Unlike the continental courts, Britain at that time made no legal allowance for "crimes of passion" or for the more modern defence of "battered wife syndrome" and so Ruth's freely given admission that she had "knowingly intended" to kill her lover fundamentally condemned her to the full rigour of the English Law, as it was at that time. Perhaps to underline this to any members of the jury that might be tempted to see Ruth as the victim, rather than the actual perpetrator the judge, Mr Justice Havers, was reported to have somewhat reluctantly disallowed the jurors from bringing back any other verdict but guilty of murder, which they duly did after 23 minutes of consideration.

With the jury's verdict announced the judge had little choice but to impose the mandatory death sentence on the 28-year-old mother of two small children who stood in the dock before him. Having received the pronouncement from Mr Justice Havers, Ruth was reported to have remained calm and thanked the judge, before turning to smile briefly at friends in the public gallery and then walked down the steps of the dock into the bowels of the court, ready for her return to Holloway Prison.

Ruth was later thought to have dismissed Desmond Cussens solicitor John Bickford and asked her own former lawyer Victor Mishcon, to look after her interests and handle any necessary letters and paperwork. The Bishop of Stepney, Joost de Blank was said to have visited Ruth in the condemned cell and reported her stating -: "It is quite clear to me that I was not the person who shot him (Blakely). When I saw myself with the revolver I knew that I was another person". De Blank was also said to be outraged when he was informed that condemned prisoners could actually hear their scaffold being constructed, although these claims were completely refuted by the Home Office, who stated that no construction work had been undertaken during the time Ruth was held there.

Unlike those who saw Ruth Ellis as a highly immoral good-time girl who should have been at home taking care of her two small children, there were many others who had a great deal of sympathy for her and unlike the English Lawmakers believed in the concept of "crimes of passion". Well over 50,000 people were reported to have signed a petition requesting the Home Secretary, Major Gwilym Lloyd George, to commute her sentence to a life sentence, which at the time was generally represented by a 12 year jail term. Despite the petition and widespread disquiet in the British media over the prospect of a young mother being hung by the state Lloyd George refused to commute her death sentence. The fact that an innocent passer-by, Mrs Gladys Yule, had been injured during the shooting was a factor in the Conservative Home Secretary's decision and the fact that the Bankers wife had not died as a result of Ellis' actions was just pure good fortune. The Tory party had also won the recently held 1955 British General Election on a strongly pro-capital punishment ticket also played a part in his decision. Had the Labour Party been elected into power, there is little doubt that Ruth Ellis's sentence would have been commuted and no doubt having served some years in prison, she would have disappeared into obscurity, never to be heard of again.

However, Lloyd George did not reprieve Ruth and along with many other supporters of the death penalty, it was said that the 28-year-old former nightclub hostess herself also welcomed his decision not to commute her sentence. Right from the outset she was thought to have accepted that she would pay for the murder of David Blakely with her own life and it was perhaps this fact alone which had engaged her thoughts over that fateful weekend, just days and hours before she finally shot him dead. Repeatedly she seems to have mentioned her own basic belief that she should pay for her crime, a life for a life and that she should not be spared the judicial cost of having killed her lover. She was even reported to have written to David Blakely's family apologising for her actions, but assuring them that she would receive final and just retribution for her crime and that was all that she could offer them as recompense for their loss.

In her final few days Ruth was said to have made a statement to her solicitor Victor Mishcom about the weekend of the shooting, confirming that she had been drinking heavily whilst in the company of an unnamed male friend and that this person had supplied her with the revolver which she used to shoot Blakely. She also recorded that this same man had driven her to Hampstead so that she could confront her lover and even suggested that he had encouraged Ruth to shoot Blakely. These were facts that had not previously been put before the court and although she had not intended for them to be used as the basis for an appeal, Mishcom finally persuaded her to allow him to use these new facts in an appeal to the Home Office. For the authorities however, these revelations provided little new information and certainly nothing that would overturn her conviction and so the appeal was rejected.

A member of Parliament George Rogers who was interested in Ruth's case tried to persuade her to make an appeal for clemency, something that she had previously refused to do and it was only after much browbeating by the representative that she was convinced to do so. However, Ruth was said to have regretted her decision almost immediately and according to the prison authorities was so upset by the events that it caused her to break down and cry, the one and only time she would show her emotions publicly. As it turned out though, George Roger's efforts on her behalf came to nothing, as the Home Secretary Gwilym Lloyd George remained opposed to granting any sort of reprieve on the basis of a "crime of passion" having been committed rather than just plain murder. Lloyd George also dismissed the argument that 'a woman was more likely to kill through jealousy than would a man'.

George Rogers would later recall his meeting with Ruth in the following way; "Here she was facing death and this had stripped her of all her feminine vanity and behaviour. She was rather thin and very pale, a rather fragile sort of person. Her eyes were shallow, with not much depth and she had a powder compact that played "La vie en rose" when it was opened"

On the day of her execution, Ruth was reported to have risen around 6.30 am and written a letter of farewell to her legal advisor Leon Simmons who had represented her at her divorce proceedings. He was said to have become so disillusioned with the British legal system following Ruth's death that he never practiced law again. At 9.00 am the door of the condemned cell was opened and Albert Pierrepoint entered the room followed by his assistant Royston Rickard and after having pinioned Ruth's arms led her without fuss to the gallows and to her enduring fame, as the final woman to be hung by the British state.

Ruth's body was left on the gallows for the stipulated one hour period, before being taken down for the mandatory post mortem to be performed, which indicated that her death had been instantaneous. Her remains were then placed in a simple wooden coffin and buried within the precincts of the prison, along with the other women who had suffered a similar fate at Holloway Prison, Amelia Sachs, Annie Walters, Edith Thompson and Styllou Christofi. Less than twenty years though, the remains of all five women were disinterred by the authorities, as the prison underwent major rebuilding work, and Ruth's body was finally reclaimed by her son Andy who was finally able to lay his mother to rest at St Mary's church in Amersham, Buckinghamshire, where she lies today under the name of Ruth Hornby.

Even from the moment that the gallows trapdoor opened beneath her feet, Ruth's execution was seen by both sides in the capital punishment debate as pivotal to their individual arguments. Those that sought to retain the punishment argued strongly that Ruth was undoubtedly guilty of the crime for which she was punished and pointed to the fact that the prisoner herself had supported the maxim of "a life for a life". Abolitionists for their part however, argued that Ruth was almost certainly provoked "beyond reason" by Blakely's rejection of her and that the loss of the baby which was thought to have been caused by the dead man's actions, could and should have been seen as a "contributory factor" in Ruth's subsequent actions.

Clearly, there was a case to be seen on both sides of the argument and the fact that Ruth seemed bound and determined to die for her crime would suggest that she had carefully weighed her actions and the likely consequences well before she pulled the trigger on that fateful Sunday evening. She was also intelligent enough to recognise that her statement in court "It's obvious when I shot him that I intended to kill him" was likely to condemn her outright and she would undoubtedly have been told that by the legal team who were trying to defend her. Some reporters have concluded therefore, that as soon as Ruth made the decision to kill Blakely, she also determined that she would die too, not as only as recompense for his murder, but also perhaps as some sort of perverted lovers pact that she alone was party to.

The tragedy of Ruth Ellis and David Blakely did not confine itself to the two protagonists themselves, but proved to have disastrous consequences for a number of their family members as well. Clearly, the Blakely family lost a son through the affair, but for Ruth's family particularly, her subsequent execution was known to have had even more catastrophic results, with her younger 18-year-old sister dying unexpectedly, reputedly from a broken heart. Ruth's former husband, George Ellis, was said to have drank himself into such a deep depression over her death that he eventually hanged himself in 1958. Her son Andy, although only 11-years-old at the time of his mother's death was reported to be emotionally damaged by her loss and carried those psychological injuries with him until his own suicide in a squalid bed-sit in 1982. Just before he took his own life, Andy was thought to have visited his mother's grave at St Mary's in Amersham and destroyed her headstone in a fit of despair.

Even those that had helped to prosecute Ruth were said to have been touched by her case, with the trial judge, Mr Justice Havers, reportedly sending money each year for Andy's upkeep and when the unhappy young man finally ended his own life in 1982, the chief prosecutor, Mr Christmas Humphrey's, was said to have paid for the cost of his funeral.

www.ingramcontent.com/pod-product-compliance
Ingram Content Group UK Ltd.
Pitfield, Milton Keynes, MK11 3LW, UK
UKHW050614260726
13967UKWH00008B/2856

9 780956 554932